FRANCHISING

FRANCHISING

A COMPLETE GUIDE FOR CANADIAN BUYERS AND SELLERS

BEV CLINE

KEY PORTER BOOKS

Canadian Cataloguing in Publication Data

Cline, Bev
      Franchising

Bibliography: p.

ISBN 1-55013-113-3

1. Franchises (Retail trade). I. Title.

HF5429.23.C58 1989   658.8'708   C89-093103-8

Key Porter Books Limited
70 The Esplanade
Toronto, Ontario
Canada M5E 1R2

Design: Denise Maxwell
Typesetting: Southam Business Information and Communications Group Inc.

Printed and bound in Canada

89 90 91 92 93 6 5 4 3 2 1

Contents

To the memory of my father, Avron Fink, who taught me about business and ethics, and then showed me how to combine them.

Acknowledgments

That this book has come to fruition is in large measure due to the help of many franchisors and franchisees across the country. To them, a large thank you. Also thanks to the many accounting and law firms for responding so promptly to the questions with which they were peppered.

Thanks also to Randy Litchfield, editor of *Small Business* magazine, for his continuous support of my work as a business journalist.

Ned Levitt, the lawyer who specializes in franchising, of the Toronto law firm Levitt, Shekter & Schnurr, as consultant for the book, has been part of it every step of the way, vetting every word from the first, bare-bones outline, to the final manuscript.

My mother, Ruth Fink, assisted me with thoughtful and insightful research and editing throughout the writing of the book.

Finally, thanks to my husband, Leigh Cline, for reading the manuscript over and over, making creative suggestions, and sharing those late-night coffees.

The chart by John Naisbitt on page 12 is courtesy of the International Franchise Association.

PART I

The Age of Franchising

Introduction

When I was growing up in London, Ontario, in the 1950s, the twice-daily journey from my home to the public school was in the order of a major undertaking. My parents, and many other parents of the baby-boom generation, had purchased land in the *suburbs* (a word always spoken with pride) only half a block from the adjoining school district. Since a major traffic artery separated our *suburbs* from the adjoining farmland, it was decided by the Board of Education that I would attend the public school the farthest, but safest walk, from our newly constructed home.

It was the kind of walk that reduced an hour-and-a-half lunch period to a frantic race to reach home, get that nutritious sandwich "down the hatch," as we said then, and race back to school in time for afternoon classes.

What made the homeward trek after school bearable were the penny candies, bubble gum and seasonal items such as wax teeth at Hallowe'en and cinnamon hearts on St. Valentine's Day, available at the neighbourhood variety stores. The store names usually incorporated those of their owners: there was Charley's, for example, which had been Joe's until Joe retired. If I saved up my allowance and totalled up the pennies, I could purchase a whole Four Liquid Flavour brand Neilson chocolate bar there. Or I could buy prepackaged black licorice strands at Flitton's, a combined grocery store and butcher shop. At every store the owners knew the children by name.

In the summers, my sisters and I would drive with my parents to the tourist town of Port Stanley, on Lake Erie. There we would float on the lake in rubber inner tubes, then drive to Shaw's, the local ice-cream factory that had the most marvellous restaurant out front.

In the 1970s I moved to Toronto. On my visits home I stopped in at the stores of my youth. Charley's was still Charley's but a new Mom and Pop operation had taken it over. Frank Flitton's store had become one of the Mac's Milk group.

There were other changes, too. The local independent hardware store, which I remembered as Plaza Hardware, had joined the Home Hardware group. A spanking new Canadian Tire had opened in the eastern part of town, near the Western Fair and Exhibition grounds, on Dundas Street, the city's main shopping thoroughfare. And Shaw's dairy in Port Stanley had expanded to become a franchisor, with convenience stores across southwestern Ontario.

In Toronto, there was evidence of a similar trend. Just a few doors away from a variety store in the city's colourful, primarily Greek area of the Danforth, I could buy any of 31 flavours of ice cream at the new Baskin Robbins outlet. Near my former home in Thornhill, the local pizza joint became a Pizza Pizza franchise. Overnight, whole playgrounds full of kids in my neighbourhood began singing the familiar "967-11-11" jingle that spelled out the central telephone ordering number.

The change of names did not necessarily indicate a change of ownership. In several cases, the family-owned enterprise was still intact. What had changed was the independent nature of each operation. Each had joined a franchise system, and while the owners were still owners, they were not entrepreneurs in quite the way they had been before.

Happily, particularly in the smaller neighbourhood

stores, the owners-cum-franchisees still knew the local children's names. But, as franchisees, they now had to conform to the standards and practices of their particular franchise system. The draw of a system with a common business format, advertising, signage and products was, in the mind of these entrepreneurs, quite simply a greatly increased chance of business success. For them, as for other franchisees, the franchise system promised strength in numbers.

I wondered what the change augured for the entrepreneur, the kind of person who used his or her own name to identify a store or service. Would such a person get lost in the mass-identity of the franchise world? Would there be room for the idiosyncrasies that made a business individual?

Franchising is definitely one of the most significant developments in current business practice. It promises, in the 1990s, to be the mainstay in the development of shopping-mall and strip-mall expansion. What does this mean for the budding entrepreneur? Just how many franchise systems are likely to succeed? And as the popularity of franchising brings new and untried franchise systems onto the market-place, just how safe will it be to invest that hard-earned cash in a franchise? In the following chapters, I have attempted to explain how franchising works, how you can get a piece of this popular pie and the pros and cons of the concept of franchising.

1

What Is Franchising?

The word "franchise" has acquired an almost magical connotation in the latter half of the 1980s. As a way of doing business, franchising seems, to the uninitiated, to promise easily obtained and unlimited economic independence.

Stripped of its magical aura, however, franchising is simply a special type of licensing arrangement employed for the distribution of products or services. A franchisor allows another person, the franchisee, to use the franchisor's intellectual property, in other words, business methods, trade marks or corporate identity, for a specified period of time. In return, the franchisee must adhere to certain standards and pay for the use of the property through royalties and/or other fees.

The Canadian Franchise Association (CFA), a 300-member lobby and educational organization, is headquartered in Toronto and has affiliates in Vancouver and Montreal. In response to calls from the public asking for an explanation of franchising and from prospective franchisors or franchisees for advice, the association has developed several publications.

In a booklet entitled *Investigate before Investing: Guidance for Prospective Franchisees*, the association starts by describing what franchising is not.

Franchising frequently and inaccurately is described as an industry or business. It is neither, but a method of doing business, of marketing a product and/or service, which has been adopted and used in a wide variety of industries and businesses [and] which has developed into an industry. Some of those businesses may have only one thing in common–a franchise system of distribution–and be very diverse in most other critical aspects.

A franchise is a contractual privilege granted by one person or company (the franchisor) to another person or company (the franchisee). The privilege granted by the franchisor to the franchisee is the right to sell, in a specified manner, a particular product or service within a specified territory. The product or service is usually identified by a trade name, trade mark, logo or other commercial symbol over which the franchisor has exclusive control.

What all this means can be illustrated quite simply. If you as a restaurant retailer want to sell Big Mac hamburgers and use the Ronald McDonald character to help promote your business, you'd better be a franchisee of McDonald's Restaurants.

The approximate cost of a McDonald's franchise at the time of writing is in the $650,000 range, a sum representing the average total investment, including the building and everything that goes into it. Also included in that figure is the nation-wide advertising and instant public recognition of a corporate identity that has been developed by the franchisor over a period of 21 years in Canada. For the sake of its franchisees, franchisors such as McDonald's fiercely guard their extremely valuable trade marks and logos.

Business-format franchising
Business-format franchising, also sometimes referred to as non-traditional franchising, with its strict adherence to a

prescribed business system and methods, is the most talked-about and fastest-growing form of franchising. It is also the type most likely to be of interest to readers of this book.

According to figures supplied to the ACF for its *Franchising '87* report, garnered from 302 completed questionnaires out of 1,070 issued to the franchise community, business-format franchising in Canada is growing at a rate of 20 percent a year. From the early 1960s, when it began to be popular in Canada, to the mid-1970s, this form of franchising expanded to represent 10 percent of all franchising. By 1987, however, close to 50 percent of all franchising in Canada was the business-format type.

Although business-format franchising is almost infinite in its varieties, it is concentrated mainly in the retail and service-industry sectors. Examples include fast food; hardware; shoe repair; hairdressing; medical, dental and legal walk-in clinics; accounting; personnel services and real estate agencies.

A franchisee who buys a business-format franchise should ideally be getting a *tried* and *true* business method. There should be detailed procedural manuals to follow, specific products to sell, and help with personnel recruitment and training, site selection, and even bookkeeping. For his or her part, the franchisee is required to conform to the format or system, maintain quality standards and pay specified fees.

There are generally three types of fees. The upfront *franchise fee* ranges from $5,000 to $50,000 and pays for the franchisor's research and development of the system, site selection and trade mark.

There is usually a monthly *royalty fee*, in the range of 4 to 8 percent, based on gross sales. However, in the case of motels, for example, these fees can be based on a straight dollar figure multiplied by the number of room nights rented out over a specified period.

Most franchisors also levy a monthly *advertising fee* of between 1 and 4 percent to pay for national advertising. Franchisees may also be asked to spend an additional 1 to 2 percent for local advertising. The product, trade mark or identifying colours–for example, the pink and blue flyers of the Molly Maid service franchise, the Golden Arches of McDonald's or the A&W Root Bear character–are designed to attract public attention to the nature of the product generally. The local advertising fee is often necessary to inform potential customers that there is an outlet of the franchise in *their* neighbourhood.

There are a few franchise groups that do not charge an upfront franchise fee or ongoing royalties. These companies are considered franchisors because they give the "franchise" to trade using a specific trade name and a specific business format. They make their money by requiring that the franchisees buy most of their products from them at a competitive, but marked-up price. Although franchisees, in this case, generally do not have to pay advertising or royalty fees, they are expected to pay outright for a specified number of flyers and other promotional materials each year. Examples of this type of franchise, although each has its own peculiarities, are the Stedmans junior department store group and the Home Hardware chain.

By purchasing a business-format franchise, the franchisee is entitled to expect (and in the case of any well-known franchisor, will certainly get) a *tested* method of doing business. Because the method has been on the market for some time, the franchisee should find that the public has faith in the particular franchise system too.

Paul Trotter, owner of Stage Sound Productions in Toronto, a sound-system rental company that provided the on-the-road sound services for the Conservative party during the 1988 election race, accompanied Brian Mulroney and his team as they made their swing through Quebec and Mulroney's Baie-Comeau riding.

"Every night after we took the system down and packed it into our trucks, the crew and I went to a St.-Hubert's Bar-B-Q restaurant to have dinner," recalls Trotter. "There was an outlet in almost every town we stopped in and we could always count on the food to be good, the service fast and the restaurants to be clean."

Trotter jokingly says that at the end of the tour he couldn't face the sight of another chicken meal, the mainstay of the franchise menu, for a full month after returning to Toronto. While this points to a drawback in the franchise concept, the limited menu offered by franchise fast-food outlets, Trotter's willingness to rely on the St.-Hubert's franchise clearly illustrates what may well be one of the strongest points in the franchise's favour in the public eye.

What brought Trotter back to St.-Hubert's was the uniformity of the business format offered by each and every outlet of the restaurant chain.

Product Franchising

Product franchising is another, much older form of franchising. Emerging at the turn of the century, product franchising once accounted for almost all franchise operations. Today, with the enormous popularity of business-format franchising, this older cousin has been eclipsed.

In product franchising, the franchisee is allowed to distribute a product, utilizing the franchisor's trade mark. This type of franchisee includes soft-drink bottlers, automobile and truck dealers and petroleum/auto service centres (gas stations).

The element common to all product franchises is a trade mark more or less widely recognized by the public.

However, in product franchising, while the franchisee must conform to standards of business as a representative of the franchisor, there is little control by the franchisor as to business methods. The franchisee is free to carry on business as he or she sees fit. In product franchising, business methods are frequently determined by the selling market and clientele.

Product franchises evolved as manufacturers and distributors realized that they needed local outlets through which to distribute their products. They also knew, of course, that by expanding distribution, they could boost product identification and so realize increased profits.

A clear example of the difference between product and business-format franchising is demonstrated by the two completely different ways in which A&W root beer is marketed.

The A&W concept began in Lodi, California, in 1919, with a sidewalk stand at which two inventors, Messrs. Allen and Wright, offered for sale a new soft drink called "root beer." Four years later, capitalizing on the growing popularity of the automobile, they opened a "drive-in" stand.

Over the next few decades, as shown by the opening of the first A&W restaurant in Canada, in Winnipeg in 1956, the inventors and their franchisees continued to refine their business concept: a drive-in restaurant at which Mama Burgers and Papa Burgers were sold with the famous root beer. In fact, the Teen Burger, the all-time favourite according to A&W statistics, proved to be even more popular than the drink as the product of choice of A&W customers.

Of course, root-beer fans who wanted to enjoy the drink had to go to one of the company's outlets to buy it. So in the 1970s the American arm of A&W decided to sell product franchises to bottling companies to bottle and distribute the product. The methods of distribution would be similar to those used to sell the bottlers' other soft-drink products.

The plan ran up against fierce opposition: A&W franchisees in the United States were so set against what they considered to be an infringement on their exclusive right to sell the product that they launched a multimillion-dollar lawsuit against the franchisor. This suit resulted in a legal settlement that secured the business-format franchisees' rights. In Canada, however, after much discussion, the franchisees agreed to allow what turned out to be a successful trial run of the soft-drink product franchise. The product distribution resulted in increased market awareness of the A&W trade mark. In 1989, A&W root beer is sold through both franchised A&W restaurant operations and through product-franchised bottlers.

In product franchising there is often more room for the entrepreneurial spirit. In business-format franchising uniformity is the key; while some franchisees complain that it amounts to blind conformity, it means that prospective franchisees who exhibit the entrepreneurial spirit to any noticeable degree are usually discouraged by reputable franchisors from joining the business-format groups.

For franchising to be successful there is very little room for individuality. The franchisee has to have enough faith in the franchisor to plunk down what is frequently a considerable amount of money and then work what usually amounts to 12- to 16-hour days in a system over which he or she has very little control.

For the franchisor who, through creativity, and entrepreneurial initiative, has put together a successful operation, franchising means reducing that operation to a set of easily understood systems. Although the franchisor can introduce new incentives, products and systems, he or she has to keep in mind that each change must be beneficial to all the franchisees in the group.

The franchisor has to realize that even though the franchise agreement may appear to give him or her the power and authority to require the franchisees to implement changes, the reality is that the franchisor must, in most cases, persuade the franchisees to make changes. This situation differs enormously from that of the business owner who merely instructs branch managers to make the desired changes.

Business is booming in the world of franchising. *The 1989 Franchise Annual*, a directory of franchisors in the United States, Canada and overseas, lists a total of 4,185 franchisors. Of this number, 1,185 are Canadian listings. (This does not necessarily mean Canadian-owned or originated, but rather that the companies operate as franchisors in Canada.)

While such a large number of opportunities may seem like a confusion of riches from which a franchisee can choose, the range of risk is wide. The 1989 edition includes 754 new listings, many of which have no track record. Chapter 4 explains how to gauge the worth of a new franchise system.

The business-format sectors listed in the Canadian section of the *Annual* are diverse and include almost any venture in which a potential franchisee could be interested:

- accounting and tax services
- advertising services
- automotive rental and leasing; muffler shops; and other automotive products and services
- building products and services
- burglar and fire protection
- cleaning services, including carpet, drapery and upholstery, maid services, laundry and dry cleaning
- employment and personnel
- entertainment, including, for example, disc-jockey services
- food products and services, including convenience and specialty stores; supermarkets; bakery and dairy products, such as donuts, cookies, ice cream and yogurt; restaurants and quick service outlets
- hairstyling and cosmetics
- health aids and services
- lawn and garden care; florists
- motels, hotels, campgrounds
- pet products and services
- photo, framing and art
- printing and copy services
- real estate services
- retail outlets selling everything from clothing, shoes and computers to electronics and video recordings
- schools and teaching services
- travel agencies

The first franchising operation, as we would define the term, began more than 125 years ago. It is usually agreed that the Singer Sewing Machine Company in the United States began to develop a modern form of franchising shortly after the end of the American Civil War in 1865. This franchise, which in those days had no descriptive tag, was a blend of today's business-format and product franchising. The Singer name brought in the customers, while the company recommended to its franchisees suitable ways to go about selling the machines. For the most part, however, franchisees were left pretty much to their own devices.

In Canada, there is no governmental body that keeps track of franchising statistics. It is estimated, however, that franchising accounts for more than $60 billion in sales annually. Over half of the retail sales in Canada are conducted by franchisees.

Sales through franchised businesses in the United States could top $2.5 trillion by the year 2010, according to John Naisbitt, author of *The Future of Franchising: Looking 25 Years Ahead to the Year 2010*, a book commissioned by the International Franchise Association.

In his book Naisbitt highlights the 10 franchise industries that he feels will have the greatest growth by 1990. Restaurants top the list, followed by non-food retailing; however, service industries, such as automotive, rental and home construction franchises, also show positive growth according to his projections.

GROWTH OF TOP FORMAT FRANCHISE INDUSTRIES 1985-1990

Business	Annual Sales (in billions)		% Growth
	1985	1990	
Restaurants (All types)	$ 48.9	$ 86.1	12.0
Retailing (Nonfood)	18.8	33.6	12.3
Hotels, Motels, Campgrounds	14.6	22.5	9.0
Convenience Stores	12.3	19.4	9.5
Business Aids and Services	12.1	21.3	12.0
Automotive Products and Services	10.6	15.9	8.5
Retailing (Food other than convenience stores)	10.2	15.9	7.0
Rental Services (Auto, truck)	5.3	8.9	11.0
Construction and Home Services	3.7	9.25	20.0
Recreation, Entertainment, Travel	1.8	6.6	29.0
TOTAL TOP TEN	$138.5	$238.1	11.5

Part of the reason for the growth is the fact that franchising is entrepreneurial in nature. In some cases, the franchisor starts the system from scratch, but generally already has a small business, often with more than one outlet.

For the independent business person, the reality of expansion is that the banks generally won't give a sufficient line of credit or an adequate loan. The banks, for their part, want their loans to be secured by assets, receivables and personal guarantees. That's when the franchisor's dreams and what he or she can reasonably secure from the bank collide.

What franchising provides for the franchisor, who often holds onto some of the outlets (called "company stores"), and the franchisees who join the system is economies of scale. Group buying-power in terms of products, location and advertising, for example, can make the franchisees' dollar go much farther than a decision to open a business independently.

The enormous number of franchise outlets springing up on every corner might lead one to believe that franchising is now the only way to conduct business. We see franchising in almost every market sector, from the most visible and extensively advertised fast-food and roadhouse-style restaurants, to motels and hotels, accounting services, hardware stores, maid-service companies and printing shops.

However, it should be made clear at the outset that to some extent the success of franchising as a method of doing business is a myth, one that originates in widely broadcast tales of a few astute or lucky owners who bought into franchise systems when those systems were in their infancy, and watched their investments soar in value when the franchises took off. Such a myth feeds on itself: indeed, franchises may succeed because their owners cannot conceive of failing.

Franchise boosters repeat tales of individuals who bought a hamburger restaurant, worked it for five years, hired a manager and then retired to live in splendour in Florida for six months of the year.

Boosters also bandy about numbers that reflect the virtual impossibility of having a new franchise fold. "Fold" is the word to watch here. When a franchise outlet is unsuccessful, it is likely to be sold to a new franchisee, not to be closed. Thus, unlike an independent business that may suddenly sport a "Going out of Business" sign, a franchise, no matter how shaky, appears to go on, possibly through the hands of a number of owners, forever. The franchisor may even take back a particular franchise and run it as a company store, rather than risk having the public get a whiff of trouble from one operation that might taint the system itself.

The claim usually made by franchise promoters is that 80 to 90 percent of newly opened franchises succeed, while a similar number of independent businesses fail.

The 80-percent success rate is probably true for new franchises *in established franchise operations*. It is certainly not the case generally. Every year as a business journalist I get several dozen calls from people who are bitterly disappointed in their franchises and are bailing out by unloading their units to new franchisees.

Most franchisees enjoy their franchises and make a living from them, but if someone sets out to buy a franchise, believing that he or she is on the road to instant riches, then he or she should forget it.

I think that the public is becoming more sophisticated in its assessment of the potential benefits of franchising. People are not leaping at every franchise opportunity that is offered. Increasingly, they are asking some hard questions about the franchisor's ideas, managerial skills and support staff available.

Says one disgruntled former franchisee of a small restaurant chain: "When there were three stores in the group owned by the franchisor, his brother-in-law and his cousin, they held family meetings over the dining table and made decisions. But when outside franchisees were brought in and the system grew, it was clear the franchisor was in over his head."

Franchising, as any franchisor or franchisee will attest, is not a substitute for hard work and that old business stand-by, time.

In essence, when all is said and done, the definition of franchising is pretty clear, believes John Johnson, national marketing manager for Kwik-Kopy Printing Canada Ltd.

In a letter sent to prospective franchisees, Johnson writes: "Most people are aware of the term 'franchising' but aren't completely familiar with what this term means. We, at Kwik-Kopy Printing, would like to clarify 'franchise' for you."

After a brief definition, Johnson goes on to give the bottom line in any business discussion: "There are only two kinds of franchises available in Canada that most people are aware of, successful ones and unsuccessful ones."

For franchising, as for any business, Johnson's comments pretty much sum up the bottom line.

Clearly, there is money to be made in franchising. For people who own several franchise outlets, the potential exists to make substantial amounts of it. But falling in love with the concept of franchising is not enough reason to hand some perfect stranger $50,000 or more and then to sign for a loan or loans that can easily total $250,000. The advantages of franchising, and its many snares and pitfalls, are discussed in Part II, with the prospective buyer, and in Part III, with the potential seller, in mind.

So You Want to Be a Franchisee?

2

The Role of the Franchisee

"Don't jump into franchising without investigating the franchise and thinking long and hard about your role as a franchisee in that system," says Norman Rolfe, senior business consultant with the Small Business Branch of the Ontario Ministry of Industry, Trade and Technology. "Don't forget that as attractive as a franchise may appear to be, this is a business relationship."

Rolfe conducts seminars on behalf of the ministry for business people thinking of buying a franchise. The seminars are offered regularly in Toronto, and throughout the province, in government buildings, community centres and public libraries. They operate as something of a travelling circus, appearing one night in Hamilton, another in London, and so on.

For a mere $15 the public can hear Rolfe, a franchise lawyer, a banker specializing in franchising and a real-life franchisee talk about all the good and bad points involved in buying a franchise. Each speaker in turn tells the audience to "investigate, investigate and investigate again before you lay down your money." Actually, admits Rolfe, the audience is probably sick of hearing that advice by the mid-point of the seminar.

All through the evening, while the experts outline how to finance the purchase, explain what to look for in a franchise document and describe a typical franchisee's day, they reiterate again and again the "investigate" advice.

Then suddenly the advice is turned inside out. "If a franchisor doesn't investigate *you* thoroughly, then you should investigate *them* even more thoroughly," Rolfe tells potential franchisees. "If the franchisor doesn't investigate you to the point that he's really sure you are a suitable franchisee for the system, then a warning light should pop on in your mind."

Even though Rolfe begins to sound like a broken record, his advice is sound, says Toula Sotirakos, a chartered accountant at Orenstein & Partners in Toronto. She has both franchisors and franchisees as clients. "Any established, credible franchisor would rather you pester him with questions about the system before you sign on the dotted line, than hear your complaints after you have paid your money and begun your training. He *really* doesn't want to hear you complain after you have opened your outlet. . . . He also doesn't want you to badmouth him."

Even after a thorough investigation on both sides, a different set of realities becomes apparent once the franchisor and franchisee start to work together.

"We have had one or two cases in which it became clear during the three-week training period that the relationship wasn't going to work out," admits Wayne Shanahan, director of operations for O'Toole's Roadhouse & Restaurants Ltd., a 58-unit (7 in the United States) franchise operation. The total investment for a franchisee to open an O'Toole's is in the $600,000 range, including approximately $200,000 of personal equity. "We felt that for the good of the entire system we had to part ways with the franchisee before we were all unhappy. Therefore we made a corporate decision to refund the $40,000 franchise fee minus a small percentage for our costs. Both parties agreed to terminate the relationship."

However, franchisees shouldn't consider the O'Toole's example to be par for the course: "Don't expect to go to a franchisor and tell him that the system just wasn't what you expected," says Sotirakos. "The franchisor would be fully justified in telling you at that point that you knew what you were getting into. He would expect you to adhere to the conditions set out in your franchise contract. It's up to you to really find out about the system before you sign the franchise documentation."

It's true, though, that many franchisees don't understand what their role in the system really is, says Sotirakos. "They understand that franchising is a business, but they don't really understand the role of the franchisor and franchisee. They really have no conception of just how intertwined the two roles really are."

"I have to admit it, we really do keep our franchisees on a fairly short lead," says Ken Kadonoff, formerly chief operating officer of O'Toole's. "We know what makes an O'Toole's restaurant work. On the other hand, there are times when a franchisee kicks and fights so hard that we let him go ahead with his idea anyway and wait to see what happens."

Kadonoff cites as an example the grand opening of the O'Toole's in Fredericton, New Brunswick. "The whole concept of O'Toole's is of a neighbourhood meeting-place where people can feel at home and like one of the gang in the style of the American local bar. Many of our customers come in wearing blue jeans.

"When we flew down to the opening of the Fredericton restaurant, we found that John Eveleigh, the franchisee licensed for the whole Atlantic provinces area, had his staff dressed in black pants, cummerbunds, formal shirts, coloured suspenders, and bow ties. We were totally flabbergasted when, [after] we remarked that it was a great idea to dress the staff that way for the big event, he told us he intended to dress them that way every night.

"His idea didn't suit the O'Toole's image," says Kadonoff. "But he insisted that his restaurant needed a more upscale image in that neighbourhood. We told him he was nuts, but sales took off and we had to admit he was right."

"A franchise concept has to be flexible enough to let a franchisee show some initiative," agrees Eveleigh. "I've made very few changes overall in my restaurant except for the attire of the staff, but my personality is such that I have to *know* that the franchisor will allow me to show some initiative."

The irony in the development of a franchise system is that when a system is young and in the first stages of development, the franchisees really want some hand-holding. As the system matures and the number of franchisees increases, the success of the system seems to give them the confidence to try to break some of the bonds.

Yet in the early stages the franchisor usually doesn't have enough confidence in the system to be able to hand-hold while struggling to first define, and then refine, the concept.

"When I bought my first franchise in 1984, O'Toole's was less than a year old and had only a few franchisees. The head office was struggling almost as hard as I was to get a grip on the tone and style of the restaurants," says David Scott. (In addition to his restaurant in Brampton, Scott purchased a second outlet in Oakville in 1988.) "In 1984, sometimes it felt like we were running on a wing and a prayer."

O'Toole's may be disposed to allow small changes, but not all franchisors feel the same way. One of the first questions a prospective franchisee has to consider, therefore, is whether he or she can handle a franchisor's saying no to a request for change in the way his or her particular outlet is run. "Ask yourself if you have the personality to completely fall in line with the franchisor's decisions," says Norman Rolfe. "This is such a serious question, that if your answer is no, perhaps you should decide to stay away from franchising or at least out of a system that maintains firm control over its franchisees."

Many franchise systems have advisory councils made up of franchisees. The key word here is *advisory*. Franchising is not a democracy. Just because an advisory council makes a recommendation doesn't mean that the franchisor has to fall into line with it.

A franchisor with some years of experience will usually at

least consider modifications to the franchise system. But, say the experts, when you sign that franchising agreement, you are in for the life of the agreement, which is usually *at least* 5 to 10 years. Don't buy a franchise expecting that you will be able to dictate what goes on in your own operation.

While the franchisor will not always act on your recommendations, you will always be expected to act on those made by the franchisor.

John Harbarenko and his wife, Helen, own two Stedmans franchises. One is in the small town of Forrest, near London, Ontario; the other in the town of Petrolia, near Sarnia.

Harbarenko has a lot of retailing experience. He worked as a general manager with the Zellers department-store chain for more than 18 years in many parts of the country. But he wanted to take what he had learned and apply it to his own business. "Coming from a retail chain, I knew how hard it is for an independent to get good pricing and a wide variety of stock, so I opted to become a franchisee. At Zellers, my efforts were going to the corporation's bottom line. Now, the profits go straight into my pocket."

Since he had so much experience in retail, his fellow dealers in southwestern Ontario asked Harbarenko to represent their region on the Stedmans Dealer Advisory Council.

Made up of 10 franchisees from across the country, the council acts as a pipeline between head office and the individual franchisees.

"One of our functions is to act as a release valve for other franchisees, so they can let off steam," says Harbarenko. "On the other hand, we also have to bring their concerns to the attention of head office.

"Most of the time Stedmans does listen to us and make the changes we ask for, but as franchisees we have to recognize that the franchisor does not *have* to bend for us."

Advisory councils and head offices can have trying times, especially when major changes are pending. Stedmans, for example, underwent a transformation in the early 1980s as it updated its fashion-buying policy and expanded into more household items so as to be more in line with competing junior department-store chains such as Kresge's, K-Mart and Zellers. It's at these trying times that the lines of communication between franchisors and franchisees have to be kept open.

Yet, no matter whether the issue is chain-wide or regional, the ultimate decision rests with the franchisor.

"I keep reminding my fellow franchisees that Stedmans doesn't have to do something the way a franchisee wants it. As a franchisee you may sometimes just have to live with something the way the franchisor has designed it," says Harbarenko.

So, if you think that perhaps you may be too independent a business person, make sure you ask franchisees currently in the system just how much freedom they have. Ask them straight out: "What happens if I refuse to do something the way the franchisor tells me to?" Then find out how disputes are resolved. Do they end up in a lawyer's office? Does the franchisor sometimes look for a compromise?

"Franchisees frequently get caught up in the excitement of franchising as a concept and don't ask the hard business questions they would certainly consider if they were opening a business on their own," says Rolfe. "They make the assumption that if the franchise is a success, then it follows like magic that they will be successful franchisees. What gets lost in the whole process is the down-to-earth basic research and evaluation of buying a particular business."

Generally franchisors expect prospective franchisees to contact current franchise owners to ask some hard questions about the franchisor, revenues, work hours, products, locations and staffing, says Rolfe.

In turn, most franchisees are willing to talk with prospective owners. They realize that the better suited a franchisee is to the system, the stronger the whole network becomes.

However, prospective franchisees should be wary of franchisees who are unwilling or unable to provide information. You have to ask yourself just why they don't want to talk with you, says Rolfe. What are they hiding? This is especially true if the franchisee doesn't want to talk with you and the outlet you are considering purchasing is *his* outlet, says Rolfe.

Rolfe advises, however, that before you start talking with franchisees, you narrow your selection to at least one or two franchise systems.

"It is perfectly all right to telephone or write to franchisors to ask for their basic information kits," says Rolfe. "Franchisors expect you to compare their outlets with those of their competition. But they and their franchisees aren't going to give you the inside story until you have satisfied them that you are really serious."

"Once we have established that a potential franchisee meets the financial and psychological criteria we require, then as a next step we suggest that he or she go meet with our franchisees independently," says John Johnson, national marketing manager for Kwik-Kopy Printing Canada Ltd. "We give the prospective franchisee a list of our outlets and three visitation cards. Then it's up to them to run down the list and pick the franchisees they'd like to have a chat with.

"We only ask that the prospective franchisee make an appointment with our franchisee rather than walking in cold," says Johnson. "It simply isn't fair to expect a franchisee to stop in the middle of what may be a large, lucrative printing order to answer someone's questions."

But Johnson stresses that a person who walks into one of the chain's outlets and asks to speak to the owner about the franchise system may be in for a rude shock. "The franchisee probably won't want to talk with you unless you have those visitation cards in hand," says Johnson. "Franchising is so popular that if the owners took the time to talk to everyone about the concept they would be neglecting their own business. Then, of course, there is the confidentiality of the system to consider."

According to Rolfe some of the questions you might consider asking the franchisee include:

1. Would you buy into the system again? If not, why not?
2. What is the total investment? Are there any hidden costs?
3. Were the financial projections of revenue, expenses and profits the franchisor gave you accurate?
4. When did the franchise make enough profit to support you? Was this in line with the time-frame the franchisor represented to you?
5. Did the franchisor live up to your expectations in training both you and your staff?
6. Was there adequate support in such areas as ongoing advertising assistance and promotion of the chain?
7. Is the product(s) of consistently good quality and were deliveries made promptly?
8. Were there any disputes? How were they handled?

Rolfe's questions about the product can be taken several steps farther. It's estimated that high-growth areas in franchising are the ones that will appeal to the baby-boom generation. This group, currently in their late thirties to mid-forties, has a high level of disposable income. They are also, despite their early years in the heyday of the turbulent 1960s, fairly settled, family-oriented consumers. They travel, eat out frequently and enjoy fixing up their homes.

But as any business person knows, tastes are fickle and economies rise and fall. The dire consequences predicted for business people and the economy after the stock market's Black Monday, October 19, 1987, did not materialize. To people who work in franchising, however, it was a reminder of how careful franchisees have to be in selecting the franchisors whose products and services they wish to represent.

Given the exigencies of the market-place, Toula Sotirakos of Orenstein & Partners says the nature of the product sold has to be a primary decision for the franchisee. Sotirakos suggests considering the following:

1. Is the product or service copyrighted or does it bear a trade mark? (Remember, part of what you are paying for when you buy a franchise is the right to a business format that includes a product or service that is widely recognized by the public.)

2. Is the product or service proved over time?

3. Is the product or service seasonal? If so, will you generate enough sales seasonally to pay your bills and support yourself over the whole year?

4. Does the product or service have mass appeal or is it limited to certain age or special-interest groups?

5. Is the product or service high-end, luxury or a basic necessity?

6. Has the product or service kept up with the competition?

7. Can the product or service be adapted to changing market preferences?

8. Can the product continue to be produced even if there are shortages of some of the key components? (This question is especially relevant for products that require specialized items, such as microchips.)

9. Are there product warranties? Who guarantees those warranties? You? The franchisor (if he or she is also the manufacturer)? An outside manufacturer? Can repairs be effected quickly to ensure the customer is satisfied quickly?

"If the products you sell in 1989 are going to be old-fashioned or hard to obtain in 1995, find another franchise system," says Sotirakos. "When you purchase a franchise the agreement usually lasts anywhere between 5 to 20 years. What are you going to do if in 5 years' time the product doesn't appeal to the public enough to make your business profitable? You might feel forced to try to get out of your agreement.

"It's far better to try to visualize the market-place over the life of the franchise agreement and purchase a franchise accordingly."

The changes that occurred in the A&W restaurant chain

during the 1970s illustrate some of the problems that can develop as a franchise responds to altered circumstances in the market.

Rumours spread quickly in small towns. In the case of Yorkton, Saskatchewan, the news in the summer of 1977 that a commercial site had been sold and a new restaurant was due to open the following year piqued everyone's curiosity. For Norm Vance, however, who had held the local A&W franchise since 1974, the news that McDonald's was coming to town was less exciting than worrisome.

In 1978 Vance's A&W was the style familiar to many restaurant-goers of the 1950s and 1960s. It was a drive-in with stalls for 60 cars. Customers sat in their cars and ordered through speakers Mama and Papa Burgers and the company's root beer. As legend would have it, pony-tailed, smiling, teenaged waitresses brought the orders on trays that attached to the top of the partially opened car window. Several generations grew up, spending their Saturday nights at the local "Dub", as the outlets were called.

But times change, and the teenagers of the 1960s and 1970s turned into the adults who were flocking to new burger chains. In Yorkton, for example, which experiences cold winters, over 70 percent of Vance's business was concentrated in the summer months. McDonald's, with its in-store seating, posed a real threat.

"Over the past 10 years A&W has poured a lot of money and time into updating operations in Canada, but in 1978, when McDonald's rode into town, the A&W operations had been pretty much the same for the past 20 years," says Vance.

Supported in spirit by his franchisor, Vance constructed a 70-seat indoor restaurant. The drive-in section still functioned, but patrons now had a choice of outdoor or indoor dining. Vance also lowered the prices of many of his items, increased his staff level and prepared, he says, "to beat the bastards at their own game." It was a case of the classic western show-down.

For the first three months during which the two fought it

out, McDonald's won hands down. "Hey, the new guy in town always has the edge," says a laughing Vance, who admits that he wasn't laughing much in those days.

Vance's situation was not unique to Yorkton, nor was McDonald's the sole competitor. As new franchise fast-food restaurants opened, A&W seemed to many to be an old-fashioned operation. In the mid-1970s the company, owned in Canada since 1972 by Unilever Canada Ltd., had sales of approximately $90 million. Today sales are in the $140-million range. The company has 240 units compared to McDonald's 550.

But back in 1978 Vance didn't care about statistics. He cared about the new guy down the block. The competition settled down after about three months and sales returned to their former level as the novelty of McDonald's wore off. Still, Vance says that he probably would have had a hard time maintaining his sales over the long haul if A&W had not modernized, by creating free-standing restaurants (a self-contained unit not attached to any other building) that sport television monitors with videos and bringing its menu more in line with current trends by introducing menu choices, such as salads and chicken items.

Vance says he would have been really dismayed when the chain went through its rocky adjustment except for the fact that A&W had many corporate-owned stores. "I knew that the people at head office had as much on the line as I did, says Vance.

So, how does it stand in Yorkton today? "Well, the McDonald's franchisee is a friend of mine," says Vance. "I think I can safely say that both our units are meeting their projections."

But what of the competitive nature of big business? "Oh yeah," says Vance, warming to the subject. "Make sure you tell everyone that we golf together and that, far and away, A&W wins on that score." Competitive spirit, never say die.

3

Why Buy a Franchise?

The reasons a person begins to think of becoming a franchisee are as varied as life itself. Franchisees, other than those who purchase a franchise in a brand-new, untested system, are usually older–at least, they are not in their early twenties or straight out of school. The upfront fee of the franchise, usually $5,000 to $50,000 isn't necessarily prohibitive: family and friends can help with that. What bounces younger franchisees right out of the picture is the total investment that they are expected to make. Generally, a retail or service franchise often translates into a total investment of at least $150,000. The franchisor wants the franchisee to have at least 25 percent of that figure, and to be responsible for securing the rest of the money. Since young people have little or no track record, that financing is hard to find.

So, the likelihood is that many franchisees are at least in their mid-thirties. By the time they have reached that age, they have been in the job market for a decade and have pretty clear ideas of their goals.

Many of these people want to have a measure of control over their lives. In many cases they have worked for large corporations and now want to carry the skills learned in big business into the challenging arena of their own small-business enterprise. One of their goals is the sense of personal achievement that independently attained success bestows on the entrepreneur.

The recession of the early 1980s, which coincided with the rise of business-format franchising, in part destroyed the myth of corporate loyalty as companies were forced to lay off trusted and valued employees. One distinct advantage that franchising has for these people is the knowledge that, even if times are hard once again, as the owners of their own businesses, they sure aren't the first in line to be laid off.

But experts warn that franchising does not offer a cure for all those who have lost their jobs, or are bored or fed up. If you hate the paperwork aspect of your present position, for example, and you buy a franchise that requires detailed reporting, then you have simply moved from the frying-pan into the fire.

Franchising lets people be their own bosses without the feeling of being adrift on the rather treacherous seas of independent business. A franchisee who has skills in marketing, for example, but not in inventory and product selection or accounting, can rely on the franchise manuals and head-office support staff to fill in the gaps. And in times of trouble, there is always the franchisor to call upon for help. (This, of course, is another reason to be very selective in choosing a franchisor—you want someone you can count on for support.)

Often the purchase of a franchise brings with it a different view of the business world or a complete career and lifestyle change.

Barry Culbert was director of marketing for Canadian Canners Ltd., the firm that manufactures and sells Aylmer and Del Monte food brands. In 1983 he decided to go into business for himself as the owner of a Goliger's Travel business franchise in Burlington, Ontario.

"My wife, Jane, and I had wanted to work together for years. We saw franchising as a chance to realize that ambition without having to open an independent business," says Culbert. "We picked the travel business partially because we felt it was a good blend of my marketing skills and my wife's administrative and computer interests and talents."

Although the recession was hurting most businesses, Culbert says that he decided to make the lifestyle change anyway. "I'm a firm believer in grasping the chance when it comes your way. Goliger's had a franchise available and we took it. I guess I figured that if I could make the business work in a bad economic climate, I'd be able to make it work any time. We had faith in ourselves and in our franchisor."

Given the fact that Culbert has purposely built up his customer base so that it is evenly divided between corporate, vacation and group bookings, he says that even should one segment of his business drop off, he still has a viable concept.

Yet contrary to public perception regarding "the sky's the limit" profits, Culbert says that currently, after six years as a franchisee, he's making about the same money he made when he left Canadian Canners. He is confident, however, that his business has a lot of untapped potential, enough to allow him to far exceed his previous earnings.

Some things haven't changed since he worked for a corporate boss: the hours he works now are just as long as they were when he was a member of the management team at Canadian Canners. Other things have changed quite a lot. He is very much aware, for example, that he no longer has a back-up team on site, as was the case before.

"When you get up in the morning and look in the mirror you realize that any goal you have set for yourself is totally up to you to achieve," says Culbert.

There are now four staff members working with the Culberts in Burlington, and the Goliger's head-office staff is in nearby Toronto, but in his old job Culbert had a whole corporate support team that met every two days to discuss ongoing business.

"Large corporate life has a different feel to it. Certainly, there's crossover in job description and function in a large company. But in your own business you wear a far greater number of hats."

For some franchisees the change in lifestyle can be far more dramatic. In fact, the changes may be so extreme that a franchisee becomes really unhappy in the new work environment. Moneysworth & Best Shoe Repair president Rick VanSant suggests that if a potential franchisee is unsure if he or she will like working with the public in a service business, it can be arranged through the franchisor that the franchisee work for a few days in one of the company's outlets.

"Generally the franchisee in our system works in his own store and that means spending much of his day repairing and doing specialized work on people's shoes," says VanSant. "Since we offer while-you-wait service, he has to be able to act quickly while being able to schedule other repairs so that the shoes are ready when people call for them later in the day."

VanSant's outlets are busy. The prospective franchisee who has thrived on long lunch hours with the gang at the office or is accustomed to leisurely social gatherings at the infamous water cooler or coffee machine may find life in a one-person store, or even one that employs one or two other persons, vastly different.

"A prospective franchisee has to be really clear in his own mind about the reasons he is buying the franchise," says VanSant. "Is he looking for a change in lifestyle, an increase in earning power or is he simply fed up in his old job?"

Consider the case of Jim Whale. Whale is a franchisee of Photo-Pet Inc., a four-year-old business whose operators have taken pictures of more than 40,000 Canadian pets, including dogs, cats, snakes, birds and guinea pigs, in their owners' homes. Photo-Pet has been franchising since 1987 and has 43 franchisees. Whale's franchise area, which takes in Bramalea, Brampton and Malton in southern Ontario, cost him only $5,000, including his photography equipment.

Given that the *total* investment for a franchise in Canada is often more than $150,000, Whale, 26, realizes how inexpensive his franchise really was. He says that he would not have considered the investment if Photo-Pet had not had a track record as a corporate entity.

"It's easy to think that a franchise is great because you can afford it, but this isn't necessarily true," says Whale, noting that most people his age cannot come up with the $50,000 or so personal equity required by more-established franchise systems. "You have to be sure that the franchisor has a business that is already up and running. Then it is for them to convince you that they can turn their corporate business into a successful franchise system."

Whale says that Photo-Pet's operation manuals, showing him how to conduct a photography business, including accounting services and central film processing at excellent bulk-rate prices, convinced him to sign on.

He admits that for the first few months he worked the franchise only at night and on weekends. He soon found, however, that any franchise, whether expensive or not, whether with one employee (in Whale's case, a woman who helps him to schedule appointments) or a hundred, requires full-time, hands-on management. Consequently, he soon gave up his secure job as a professional electrical wireman.

"It became clear early on that I could run this as a rinky-dink additional income or I could go into business properly," says Whale. "I wanted it to be more than a supplement to my regular income."

Whale's life has changed dramatically, he says. Gone is the paycheque every two weeks. Instead there is the unrelenting paperwork that goes with every business, the considerable challenge of keeping his equipment in working order, and the stress brought on by having to rely on his own wits and ingenuity in order to prosper. His own working hours have changed as well. Whale finds that the majority of his appointments are at night and on the weekends.

Whale estimates that his business will gross $80,000 in its first fiscal year. In most other franchise systems a 15 to 20 percent bottom line is considered acceptable; Whale's will be much higher. His business format does not require an office; because he can work out of his home, his overheads are correspondingly low.

Of course, one of the prerequisites of his business is that he have the patience of a saint in dealing with other people's pets.

"People talk about the challenges they have in the office," says Whale. "My biggest problem recently was with a tortoise. He kept running off the table every time I reached to pick up a piece of driftwood to position him on. Every time I turned around he was off and running." He laughs. "I guess you could say that my life has changed dramatically since I decided to become a franchisee."

4

Checking Out the Franchise Opportunity

Some people tend to fall in love with the idea of franchising, according to Bernie Webber, assistant deputy minister, Ontario Ministry of Consumer and Commercial Relations, Business Practices Division. Webber calls himself "the guy who has to write to people to tell them they got taken, or that they can bitch all they want but that their franchisor is right and legal according to the franchise agreement."

Unfortunately, people tend to call his office *after* they have invested their money and come to grief. The prospect of making a great deal of money for a capital outlay of, say, $25,000, for a franchise outlet is often irresistible. At first glance, the attraction can be overwhelming: the capital outlay is low compared to the cost of setting up an independent business; specialized training may be provided, together with access to proven marketing techniques; and the franchisee enjoys support in the form of broad-based advertising programmes and well-designed support accessories, such as uniforms and give-aways.

"What is more difficult to grasp is that each of these values has a high price. After a few years, your ingenuity will suggest changes and these will be stifled. You will spot a more attractive location. Your volume will go up because you work hard [then] suddenly your rent will increase because your business is more valuable than before. Or suddenly [you will find that] your territory is no longer sacred," says Webber. Then the complaints begin.

Webber emphasizes that prospective franchisees *must* investigate the limits of their franchise agreement: "Do not get yourself emotionally 'sold' before you seek independent legal advice. You may think you'll be your own boss [Isn't that what so many franchising advertisements say?] but our enquiry files tell a different story!"

According to the Ontario Ministry of Industry, Trade and Technology and the management consulting firm Woods Gordon, there are a number of ways to check out a franchise opportunity. Their suggestions in an expanded format include the following:

1. *Write to each franchisor who interests you and ask for a franchise kit.* If there are several franchisors in an industry sector that interests you, write to all of them, so that you can compare what they have to offer. If one franchisor is asking for an upfront fee of $10,000, and another for $25,000, then you should ask the more expensive one just what extra, and perhaps necessary, support services you will receive for the additional money.

2. *Ask for the franchisor's most recent financial statement, showing profit and loss.* Ask for a pro-forma statement (projected financial statement). Also get the names of the principals of the company so that you can check them out. Do not be embarrassed to ask for this information. This is your financial future you are talking about.

If the company is public, the information is easy to obtain, usually straight from the company itself. However, if the company is small and does not want to give you the pertinent details, make sure to check with the Canadian Franchise Association or the Better Business Bureau in both the franchisor's head-office city and your city.

Check the company's financial and/or pro-forma statements with a lawyer and accountant who *specialize* in franchising. Your family lawyer may know all there is to know about your will or your real estate holdings, for example, but franchising is a relatively new specialty, and you want to get the best advice available.

Your investigation may take some time. You may have to wait while your request for information is processed and returned to you, but you shouldn't be in too much of a hurry to sign on the dotted line in any case. If, for example, a franchisor tells you that only one franchise is available in a given area, and that if you don't sign today you might lose the deal, then it might be better to walk away. In one case I know of, a prospective franchisee lost a $10,000 non-refundable deposit because the franchisor insisted that the deal be signed immediately. The prospective franchisee's lawyer was on vacation and he was so eager to sign that he handed over the money directly to the franchisor instead of waiting for his lawyer to return or giving the deposit to another lawyer in trust.

3. *Check to see if the franchisor is operating in Alberta or in the United States.* Franchisors operating in these areas are required by law to prepare disclosure statements (financial statements and information on the principals involved), which are available for you to look at. (For more information about Alberta's regulations, see later in this chapter.)

4. *Ask for a copy of the franchisor's trade-mark application or registration.* If the trade mark is unprotected, it means that you and the franchisor may have difficulty in preventing unauthorized persons in competition with you using the trade mark. In such a case, the franchise is almost without value.

5. *Request a list of other franchisees in the system.* Do not accept an abbreviated list that lets the franchisor choose to whom you will speak. If you are considering buying a

resale (see Chapter 12) make sure to ask both the franchisor and the franchisee why that unit is being sold. Even then, talk to other franchisees in the system as well.

Select a range of franchisees to talk to. From one who is new to the system you want to discover how good the franchisor's support is currently; from one who has been in the business for a few years, you want to know if the financial projections are accurate and if the franchisor support is consistent; and in talking to a long-term franchisee who has watched the system evolve, you should ask what pitfalls you might experience and how they can be avoided.

You should also try to talk to a franchisee who operates in an area comparable to the one you are considering. After all, there is no point in comparing an outlet in St. Thomas, a small town in rural Ontario, to one in downtown Montreal.

6. *Complete the application process and be prepared to disclose your financial background.* You should be seriously concerned if the franchisor is not interested in your credit and work history, for example. Too much eagerness to recruit you may be a sign that your upfront funds are required to buoy up a sagging system. Bear in mind that a new franchise system will have to be operating for as long as four or five years before the royalties are flowing in sufficient volume for the franchisor to make a significant profit.

7. *Obtain a full set of legal documents.* These should include the franchise agreement and any leases or subleases that you will be required to sign. Take them to a franchise lawyer.

8. *If you are required to give a deposit, ensure that it is refundable.* If it is not refundable, make sure you can get at least 80 to 90 percent back. The remaining money may be used by the franchisor to check you out, scout for prospective sites for you or to do market or demographic studies of the area you are discussing.

9. *Analyse the proposed site very carefully*. Ask for the studies the franchisor has undertaken that prove that a franchise will have a good chance of success in that area.

10. *Visit the actual building and note the surrounding types of businesses*. Make sure that the building can accommodate your kind of business and that you will feel comfortable in that community. For major investments over $100,000 you may want to call in an architect to confirm that any modifications that the franchisor has proposed to make to the building can actually be made.

11. *Talk over the prospect of buying a franchise with your family*. In the early life of a new franchise (as opposed, for example, to a resale) the franchisee may have to work long hours to get the business established. Are you prepared to sacrifice a significant portion of your family life in order to get the franchise off the ground? Is your family prepared to accept your frequent absence from home?

You may have to move to a new city or neighbourhood in order to purchase a franchise. The Molly Maid cleaning-service franchises, for example, are all sold out except for 10 or 15 territories in western Canada. And Stedmans stores are located only in small towns of under 10,000 people. So, if you have your heart set on a particular, successful franchise, or if you are accustomed to big-city life, you and your family may have to be prepared for a major change in your way of life. Does your spouse really want to make that dramatic a change? Are those services your family considers essential available in the new location?

12. *Take a day or two to review the pros and cons*. It is easy to get caught up in the excitement of embarking on a new direction in life. Apply as much common sense as possible to this important business decision. If you feel confident, proceed. If not, let this particular opportunity go. Even if, for example, you like the franchisor but not the location, resist the temptation to sign. A reputable franchisor will not fault you for declining a particular location.

Although most franchisors are ethical, the world of franchising, too, has its fast-talking scam artists. In the best of all business scenarios, you plunk down your upfront fees and get a viable business plan and solid support from a franchisor. You work your unit, sell it for a good price and then retire in comfort. But for the unwary, there are pitfalls in this dream-world scenario. There are actually very few real scam artists in Canada who make a living by running off with your money, mostly because of experiences in the United States through the 1950s and 1960s that led to disclosure and other franchising legislation.

In those decades "getting into a franchise" became the goal of thousands of Americans, and franchise fever led to wild abuses. Many gullible movie stars and entertainment persons lent their names to franchising concepts, but had no other connection with the system. When many of these systems, based only on getting upfront fees, failed, legislators moved in to clean up the industry.

A famous case in the late 1960s was the Minnie Pearl chicken franchise, which was promoted as a good investment because of its supposed link to the country-music singer. Thousands of people flocked to put down their money. Many of these outlets never even opened, and none of them survives today.

In contrast, franchising in Canada during those decades was too small an industry to attract scam artists. There have been, however, several documented cases of less-than-honest franchise promoters in Canada. One particularly well-known Canadian case concerns a promoter, Melvin Deutsch, who collected fees for a franchise system in which not a single franchise unit was built or opened.

In a story that appeared in *Small Business* magazine in December 1986 a team of journalists, including myself, Randall Litchfield, Catherine Kentridge and John Twigg probed the story of Burger World, a hamburger franchise that would use robots programmed to run along special tracks and stop at tables to deliver food orders. In 1981 and 1982 Deutsch, as a representative of Global Franchise Marketing Ltd., sold franchises for the chain. The brochure and marketing package contained elaborate plans for the stores and claimed that the first outlet would open soon in Sarnia, Ontario.

Not only were no units built, but when investors asked for their money back, they were refused. As a result, a businessman who had invested $128,000 in the scheme asked the Supreme Court of Ontario to declare the company bankrupt and appoint a trustee of its property. The court complied in a 1982 trial and awarded all costs to the businessman. At the time the judge said that Global's operation had "all the earmarks of an escalating fraud" and that Global's officers had "deliberately misled the petitioning creditor and others."

Although Deutsch was only one principal officer of Global it came as a shock in 1986 to see him, under the guise of a new company, Deutsch McCormick D'Amato & Associates (DMD), promoting Burger World franchises again through newspaper advertisements. In an interview I conducted with Deutsch, he told me that the outlet would soon be open in Sarnia, as in the intervening five years the company had found a way to solve the problems with the concrete floor and the tracking mechanism. He also said that Paramount Studios in California had purchased a Burger World franchise to operate on its lot to serve a dual purpose—as a movie set and as an actual restaurant. But Paramount told the team there was no Burger World at their studios.

Deutsch undoubtedly signed on more franchisees in the few months between the newspaper ads of September 1986 and our story. In fact, he was selling the rights to develop franchises in specific areas for $5,000. When the team contacted the Vancouver-area franchisee, for example, he was shocked at what we told him about the history of the company. He said he would contact his lawyer and, immediately, if the facts were as we had presented them, he would jump ship.

Then there's the case of a promoter I'll call Fast Freddie (I can't use his real name as he has not been charged with any offence). Freddie shows up at most franchise-opportunity fairs and trade shows to promote his pizza concept. Each time, the concept has a different name, trade mark and logo. There's a good reason for these changes. Several months after each show, also after prospective franchisees have put down their $10,000 nonrefundable deposits, Freddie figuratively throws his arms up in the air and announces that the system has failed. The franchisees are out of luck and out of pocket. After all, claims Freddie, his isn't the first system to be unsuccessful.

Increasingly, people are calling for more comprehensive disclosure rules. However, the fear is that as a consequence the industry could become over-regulated and unwieldy. Under the current rules we can be thankful that there are few out-and-out scam artists.

Yet, since there are no disclosure rules and any franchisor can literally hang out a sign and set up shop, we have attracted numerous well-meaning, but inept franchisors. These people might have a good product or a good idea, but are incapable of setting up and running a viable franchise system. An inept franchisor, however well-intentioned, can still cost a franchisee his or her entire investment. The franchisor may be the nicest guy in the world, but the franchisee of a bankrupt system will still face the consequence of not having adequately researched his or her credentials.

The Case of Alberta

Alberta is the only province that requires registration, and disclosure of certain information, before a franchisor can begin to sell franchises to the public.

Anyone who sells or offers for sale a franchise for money or other assets is considered to have made a "trade," according to Bob Demcoe, chief of securities administration for the department of the Alberta Securities Commission that administers the Alberta Securities Act. And with some exceptions those who make a trade in Alberta must file an application for registration and a prospectus.

At that point, says Demcoe, commission staff vet the prospectus to make sure the paperwork meets their criteria. Until the franchisor receives a receipt to show the vetting is complete, he or she may not begin to sell franchises.

"What we are looking for is full, true and plain disclosure," says Demcoe. "We are trying to protect the consumer who is thinking of purchasing a franchise. Many of these files are made available to [members of] the general public, who can just walk off the street to examine them."

The prospectus contains such information as a general description of the business, the most recent financial statement and the proposed franchise agreement.

If the franchise system is new, and therefore has no track record, the franchisor must make that fact clear in the prospectus and alert the reader to the risks involved with a new system.

However, an established franchisor who has a consolidated net worth of $5 million, and has operated 25 or more franchises in the past five years, can ask to be exempted from filing the prospectus, says Demcoe. Except in rare cases in which it is felt that allowing the franchisor (one who has been around a long time and has a good track record in other parts of the country) to trade in Alberta without the required paperwork would not be harmful to the public, the franchisor must file a Statement of Material Fact.

This filing includes such information as the name of the franchisor, the franchisor's agent in Alberta, the franchise agreement and specifics such as the termination and renewal terms.

Even though the information exists in Alberta, I have found that not a single disgruntled franchisee I have spoken to had checked with Alberta before signing the franchise agreement. Since the information is readily at hand, take advantage of it. Remember, check, check and recheck the franchise opportunity before you sign.

5

Fees and Royalties

Almost all franchisors have front-end fees that a franchisee pays on joining the system. These fees can range from $10,000 to more than $25,000.

The front-end fee is not, contrary to the expectations of some new franchisors, meant to pay for expansion of the franchise system, but to pay for the costs of the development of the new franchisee's business and all the attendant support systems the franchisor offers.

Kwik-Kopy Printing Canada Ltd. charges $49,500 as a front-end fee. There is a 10 percent reduction if the franchisee pays cash; Kwik-Kopy will finance up to $20,000.

The total investment in a Kwik-Kopy franchise is approximately $128,500, comprising the front-end fee and a bank package of $79,000, according to national marketing manager John Johnson.

For his or her total investment the franchisee gets a "turnkey" operation: the unit is built and ready to open its doors for business (there is even a $100 float in the cash drawer). Also included in the price are such support items as operating manuals; three weeks of training at the company's corporate headquarters in Houston, Texas; a completely set-up computer system and programmes; and the services of three Canadian head-office trainers who work with the franchisee for several weeks just prior to and after the opening of the store.

Franchisees seldom complain about the front-end fees or the cost of their total investment. But frequently the franchisor and franchisee may not see eye to eye on the royalty payments that form the basis of a franchise system.

In service-based franchises in which the business is often run from home, the front-end fees are much lower. Molly Maid, for example, charges only $11,000. This fee is for the use of the trade mark and the business format only, since there is no physical location that requires the franchisor to do site evaluations, set up head leases (they usually sub-lease to their franchisees) and hire construction companies.

In almost all franchise systems (Stedmans is an exception as the company makes its money solely by wholesaling products to its retailers), there is a royalty fee charged on gross annual sales for the use of the trade mark and the system methods. The fee ranges from a low of 3 or 4 percent to as much as 10 percent. In addition, there is often an advertising fee ranging from 1.5 to 3 or 4 percent that in reputable franchise systems goes into a completely separate pot to be used solely for advertising.

The advertising fee is usually based on gross annual sales, but can be capped. Kwik-Kopy franchisees, for example, pay a 6 percent ongoing royalty rate, but the top figure for advertising is $12,000 per unit. This means that a very successful franchisee does not bear a disproportionate share of the advertising budget. Similarly, Goliger's head-office personnel meet with their franchisees several times a year to decide on a flat-rate advertising figure. "In the travel business we have times of the year that we need to do much heavier advertising," says franchisee Barry Culbert. "We apportion the money seasonally and make sure that all the franchisees in the system pay their fair share."

Franchisees grow irate when they form the idea, rightly or wrongly, that their ongoing royalty is not being used to support them. "The franchisee depends on the franchisor for help in areas such as marketing, new-product development, supplier sourcing, site design and development, accounting systems, computerization, upgrading courses and field support," says Toula Sotirakos of Orenstein & Partners. "If the franchisee feels that help is there when he asks for it, he doesn't mind paying the royalty."

But new franchisors often underestimate the large amount of help an equally new franchisee requires, says Sotirakos. In such cases the franchisee is resentful right from the start about the money he or she is remitting on a regular basis to the franchisor.

As the franchise system matures, the demands of the franchisees increase. "When I bought my first O'Toole's franchise, my training period consisted of little more than a tour of an existing O'Toole's restaurant, and a demonstration of how to make a chef's salad," says franchisee David Scott. "Today the training programme is three weeks long and takes you through every step of being a restaurateur. O'Toole's costs have escalated dramatically, but so has their level of service."

While a franchisee will not see head-office personnel on a daily or weekly basis, especially if the system is large (more than 50 outlets), one of the prerequisites of a good franchise system is to have adequate head-office personnel.

Kwik-Kopy Canada has nine staff members in the "support section" of its operation. This does not include other head-office staff who work in accounting, franchisee selection or site development according to Dennis Crisp, vice-president of operations.

Kwik-Kopy's support-management structure is illustrated opposite. What is particularly interesting is that, as the illustration shows, separate Kwik-Kopy staff are hired to support the franchisees. A different administrative team handles product sourcing and advertising for the franchise group.

KWIK-KOPY MANAGEMENT STRUCTURE

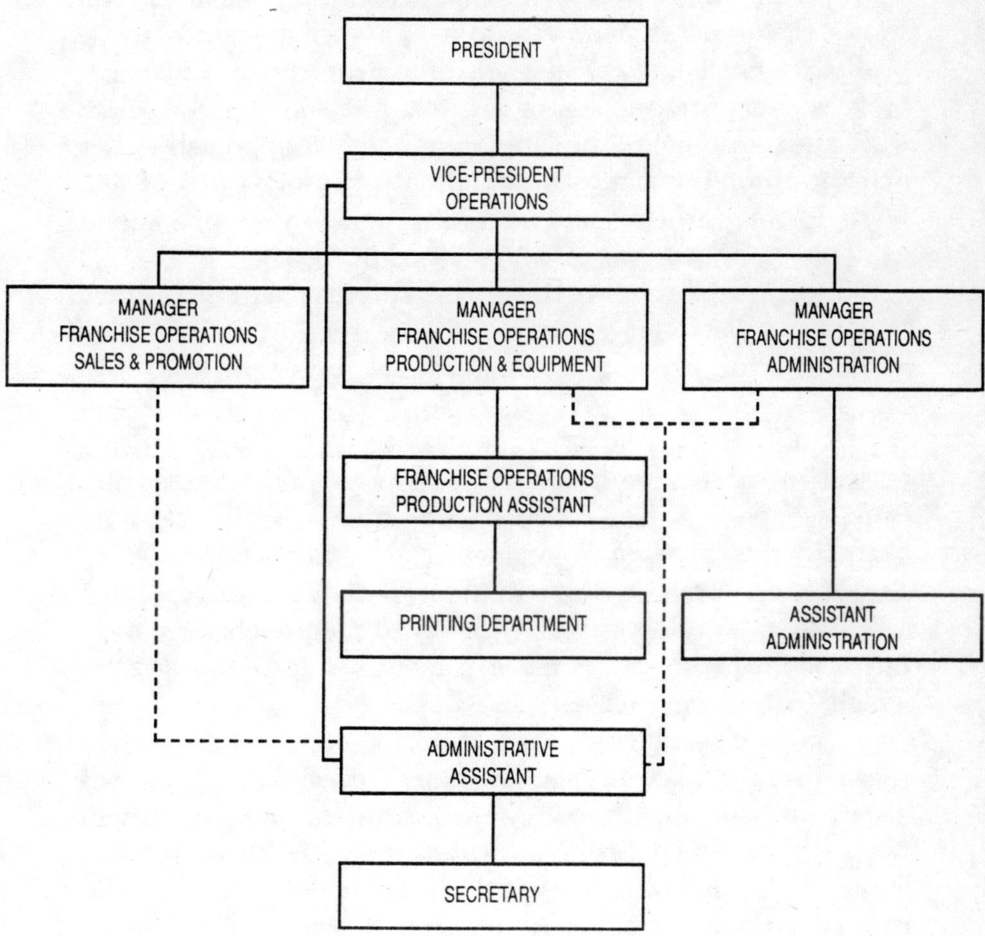

"When a new franchisee has completed his training in Houston, our people in Toronto take over the local support," says Crisp. "Two weeks before the outlet opens, the field manager in charge of production helps the franchisee interview the press operators and set up the equipment. Then, the next week the field manager of administration comes in to set up the computer system with the accounting packages, and shows the franchisee how to price in such a way as to be profitable. Finally, the week the store opens, the field manager of sales and promotion goes out into the local market-place with the franchisee, showing him how to approach other neighbourhood businesses for their printing and copying work. He helps the franchisee to utilize the knowledge gained in the training sessions down in Houston."

Field managers also travel the country, setting up new franchise outlets, but a large portion of their time is taken up working with existing franchisees on problem areas, says Crisp.

A different group of employees handles the advertising budget in most large-scale franchise systems. In the smaller systems there may not yet be enough money to hire separate staff, but the money is segregated from the royalty funds.

Moneysworth & Best's founder, Rick VanSant, says that advertising not only brings customers to the franchisee's door, but also helps to bring more franchisees into the system, which, in turn, strengthens it.

VanSant says he uses the advertising budget to make shoe repair more upscale in the consumer's eyes. The company's advertising campaign, showing a woman wearing a pair of high heels with one heel broken, sported the line, "Bring us your wounded." VanSant says that the objective of all the company's advertising is to reposition shoe repair in the market-place. "Historically, people let their shoes run down to the point that they have to throw them away," says VanSant. "We want people to think of shoe repair as a viable alternative to reinvesting in new footwear."

Since franchisees contribute to the advertising for the

system, they want to have a say in it. Several years ago, Kwik-Kopy decided to launch a magazine called *Kudos*. The magazine carried stories of successful entrepreneurs (not necessarily in the Kwik-Kopy system), gave business-to-business hints and celebrated the spirit of small business.

But the franchisees felt that the magazine wasn't doing enough to promote the Kwik-Kopy concept, says John Johnson. "They felt their money would be better spent on advertising that encouraged people to come into a Kwik-Kopy outlet. So the magazine was dropped."

Similarly, Goliger franchisee Culbert, who sits on the chain's advertising council, says that the franchisees want to be consulted. "One of the most successful promotions we had was a nationally televised contest we conducted with the Home Hardware chain [also a franchised operation]. As a franchisee I felt the campaign brought me a lot of recognition. I would vote for that kind of campaign again."

"Vote" may be the operative word. Including franchisees in advertising decisions is necessary, agrees Sotirakos. "If you are asking your franchisees to contribute to the fund, you'd better be prepared to listen to what they feel will work in their market areas," says Sotirakos. "At the head-office level it is easy to get out of touch with what is happening a thousand miles away."

6

Financing

Many potential franchisees get a real shock when they realize that the franchisor expects them to make a hefty equity commitment toward the total cost of their new business.

Generally franchisors like to see the franchisee come up with at least 25 to 50 percent of the total investment. This includes such costs as the research and development of the site, construction, stocking the outlet with inventory and working capital.

"The franchisor wants to be sure that the franchisee has a personal stake in the business," says Norman Rolfe, senior business consultant with the Small Business Branch of the Ontario Ministry of Industry, Trade and Technology. "The difference between a corporate-owned store and a franchise is that [in the franchise] there is an *owner-manager.*"

A second shocker is that the franchisor expects unencumbered money. If a franchisee owns a house that is mortgage free, for example, the franchisor might allow the franchisee to obtain a large mortgage on the home as part of the franchisee's equity. However, if the franchisee intends to work the franchise with his or her spouse, the total family income would be derived from the franchise outlet and the franchisor might not approve the deal.

"The last situation a franchisor wants is for the franchisee to be so financially strapped that his attention is diverted from running the business," says Rolfe. "Franchisors really prefer the franchisee to have completely unencumbered money."

Once the franchisee has been accepted into the system, however, there are many cases in which there is no need to search for a lender from whom to borrow the money for the rest of the investment.

Often franchisors will arrange for a lending institution to offer franchisees a package particularly suited to the initial capitalization and the ongoing requirements of the system.

One such franchisor is The Angelo Corporation, which operates the Signor Angelo and Madame Angelo fashion-accessory retail stores.

"We don't demand that a franchisee get his financing from the bank we deal with, which is the Canadian Imperial Bank of Commerce," says Sam Karmali, vice-president, finance. "The franchisee is free to tell us that he already deals with 'so-and-so' at a specific bank and that he prefers to continue banking there. But if the franchisee doesn't have an ongoing relationship with a particular bank, we suggest he consider the CIBC package.

"The bank is already familiar with our stores. The banker, whether in Surrey, British Columbia, Winnipeg or Ottawa, knows our background, assets and the potential of our stores, so the franchisee doesn't have to come up with a lot of information about the system. The franchisee has only to furnish his own personal information.

"Having a franchise services package means that the franchisee receives consistent and prompt service through any one of a bank's branches," agrees Charles Scrivener, manager of the franchising section of the Independent Business Division of the CIBC.

"Once the office of Signor Angelo has approved a franchisee, they inform a predesignated regional officer who is part of our Regional Franchise Marketing Group, and give us the name and telephone number of the franchisee. At the same time, Signor Angelo provides this officer with a package containing financial projections for that particular store and details of the assets to be financed.

"In turn, the regional manager passes the information to the branch manager who will be the one to eventually handle the franchisee's account," says Scrivener.

One of the advantages of this system is that the manager already has a copy of the franchise service package that Signor Angelo has set up with the bank and has a good understanding of the particular franchise concept.

This process ensures, first, that the franchisee is referred to the appropriate lending officer, says Scrivener, and, second, that the franchisee doesn't have to waste time explaining the franchise concept and can get on to the pertinent financial discussions.

Karmali says that his chain created the package with the CIBC as an added facility for their prospective franchisees. "The more we as a franchisor can offer our franchisees, the greater our support of their efforts," says Karmali. "We all know that financing can at times be difficult to obtain."

Still, any bank that is approached has to be convinced that the franchisee fulfills the lending conditions. The franchisor can prequalify all he wants, but whether or not financing is obtained is the bank's judgment call.

While it isn't the banker's responsibility to vet prospective franchisees, and such considerations may not be in the front of the banker's mind when evaluating individual applications, it stands to reason that the banker who handles a lot of the franchisor's business will want to ensure that each franchisee is capable of running the outlet.

"Just as with any other business transaction, we have to be convinced that the franchisee's application is sound enough to consider granting the loan," says Terry Myers, manager of franchise banking services in the Commercial Financial Services Division of the Toronto Dominion Bank. Myers works with franchisors to draw up financing packages tailored specifically to the requirements of a particular system.

However, the three-cornered relationship between the

bank, franchisor and franchisee doesn't end there. Even after the loan is granted, the franchisee usually signs a form allowing the bank to release information about the business to the franchisor at regular intervals. This is a rather interesting banking concept. Generally, banks are reluctant to provide client credit information even when a client gives the bank as a reference for credit purposes. However, franchisees routinely sign legal papers allowing the bank to disclose information to the franchisor. The theory is that for the greater good–in other words, for the good of the entire franchise group–the franchisor needs to know if there are any weak links in the chain. Presumably if some operations are less profitable than others, or if one operation is in definite trouble, the franchisor can come to the franchisee's assistance.

While some franchisees don't like this Big Brother-like intrusion into their financial affairs, most are reluctant to discuss their objections publicly. Says one franchisee: "Allowing the bank to disclose my private business to my franchisor tends to make me look over my shoulder even when I am doing well. I don't like the lack of privacy. But this is one of the prices I pay for being a franchisee."

This franchisee admits that, given his desire for privacy, he could have arranged his financing at a bank other than the one that handles the franchise package. But then again, he is not so sure that he would have been approved.

"The bank knows the franchisor and knows that the franchisor has a good reputation for straightening out problem franchises. So, I think the bank is perhaps slightly easier in making credit available to franchisees."

Despite what some may see as a Big Brother approach, openness between the franchisor, franchisee and bank has positive benefits for all concerned, according to spokesmen for the banks.

"In theory the franchisor, franchisee and the bank act much like a three-legged stool," says Terry Myers. "We act together to make sure the franchisees are funded, but we also know if a franchisee has a financial problem."

In a franchise system, a franchisor's worst nightmare is to

suddenly find one of his outlets closed for financial reasons. To customers, one closed outlet may signal a problem with the entire chain, when in reality it is only one franchise that is in trouble. Yet, just as in an independent business, the bank, if required, can step in and close down a franchised outlet.

A franchisor who is fully informed about the financial situation of his or her franchisees can plan for this eventuality, according to Myers. If a franchisor has a good relationship with the bank, action can be taken to keep a franchisee afloat, or, in the worst case, the head office can take over the store until a new franchisee is installed.

"In the best of all possible worlds, the system should work to the benefit of the bank, the franchisor and the franchisee so that there is enough money to fund the business initially, and then to help it grow to become a viable entity," says Myers.

One company that has worked out a package for its franchisees with the Toronto-Dominion Bank is St. Clair Paint & Wallpaper Ltd., a publicly traded company listed on the Toronto Stock Exchange. The company has been in the paint, wallpaper and home-decorating business since 1939, but began selling franchises in 1970. There are currently 195 retail stores, 49 of them company-owned.

According to Tom Fischer, vice-president, finance, the total investment for a unit varies from $140,000 to $180,000, depending on whether the outlet is free-standing or in a mall (in which rents are usually quite high).

The company expects prospective franchisees to have a full 50 percent of the total investment in unencumbered money. "We realize that many other franchisors allow franchisees to invest much less in the operation, but we want to be absolutely certain that our franchisees can handle their debt load," says Fischer.

In the chain's shopping-centre outlets, for example, the costs would break down as follows: franchise fee, $20,000; furniture, fixtures and equipment, $40,000 to $60,000; leasehold improvements, $40,000 to $60,000; inventory, $55,000; and advertising and grand-opening costs, about $5,000.

Since the least amount the franchise can cost, given these expenses, is $160,000, the franchisee must come up with a minimum of $80,000, says Fischer. The rest is financed, upon credit approval, through the Toronto-Dominion Bank. The loans are made up of a combination of commercial loans and the so-called Small Business Loan (see below). The bank also offers, for a fee, computer payroll services and on-line access through computer to account balances.

Given that St. Clair Paint & Wallpaper strives to prevent franchisees from getting in over their heads by swamping them under heavy debt servicing, Fischer figures that an average free-standing store that generates, perhaps, $450,000, or a mall outlet with sales in the $1 million range, can likely allow the franchisee to pay back his or her loan in three or four years. The franchisee could also reasonably expect a pretax profit of $20,000 to $80,000 after all salaries, including a franchisee's own salary of $30,000 to $35,000.

Still, whether or not a franchisor has put together a package with a bank, there are some basic rules to be observed in dealing with a bank, according to Jack Hertzberg, accountant in the franchise business services of Price Waterhouse in Toronto, a national accounting and consulting firm.

"Do your homework and develop a loan presentation and business plan that leaves no questions unanswered," says Hertzberg. At a minimum Hertzberg's plan which is expanded below, should include:

1. *An overview of your financing requirements*. If the total investment is $250,000, and you are putting up $60,000, for example, then you should note the total amount of money required immediately, and the amount required after you open. Break down the total to show what portion is for each of the upfront fee, construction of the premises, leasehold improvements, stocking of inventory and initial training and staff costs.

Include a complete list of each projected cost, including such items as leasehold improvements (alterations to leased premises), signage, telephone, advertising, stationery and promotional items. Be sure to include the costs of financing (i.e., interest payments).

2. *Business description*. Detail the nature of the business. For example, is it a fast-food outlet, leisure business or home-cleaning service? Describe the product and why it is likely to be successful. Explain how the business works (the business format). Give some history of the franchisor's experience, management and support programmes.

3. *Market analysis*. Before you get to the stage in which you are looking for financing, you or your franchisor should have prepared a market analysis of the business in the proposed geographic area. This analysis should include such items as the demographics and the potential competition. In other words, you are looking for information that outlines particulars such as the age group and income level of the people who live in the area you will be servicing. Most major accounting firms and specialty market-research firms can furnish you with information and an analysis. It is also possible to get basic information from Statistics Canada.

4. *Personal résumé*. Your bank will want to see a résumé that outlines your education and work history. They will look for evidence of personal stability and a stick-with-it attitude. Include your marital status (the bank will want to know that your spouse is supportive and behind you all the way) and the number of your dependants. Indicate whether your spouse is going to work in the business, and, if not, the salary range of your spouse. The bank will want to know how the family income will fare during the time it takes the franchise to become profitable. Make sure you include both personal and business references, and be prepared to have the bank call those people.

5. *Personal statement of net worth*. The bank will ask to see a list of all liabilities and assets. This includes items owned, such as a house, car or boat, and the amount still owing on each item. The bank will want to know of ongoing liabilities, such as credit-card balances, leases and

monthly remittances for such items as life insurance. The bank will then work out a debt-to-equity ratio (in other words, the percentage of what you owe in relation to what you own) and judge whether taking on more debt in the form of the loan to buy the franchise is reasonable. Their concern (and surely yours, too) is that you not have so many debts already that you cannot afford to wait out the unprofitable startup period before drawing a salary.

Include a list of all the unencumbered capital that you have available to invest. This includes money that you can lay your hands on without borrowing against an asset. Common items include cash, stocks and bonds, real estate or automobiles. Then figure out, if necessary, what you can reasonably mortgage.

6. *Security and repayment terms.* The bank will ask how you intend to repay the loan. Is your business seasonal? If so, do you propose to pay increased principal payments, for example, during high-sales, high cash-flow periods? Do you require small repayment terms during the first year of the business to allow for growth?

The bank is likely to ask for your personal guarantee for the loan, and may ask that your spouse sign a personal guarantee as well.

The assets of the business, including furniture and fixtures, may be pledged against the loan. As outlined in your franchise agreement, inventory may be subject to a buy-back to the franchisor. Alternatively, it may form part of the security guarantee. Often the franchisee will agree to pledge the accounts receivable as a guarantee against the loan.

7. *Financial forecasts.* Draw up a forecast showing where you expect your sales, expenses and profit figures to be over the next year, two years and five years. This will help the bank to determine the rate of payback and decide whether the amount of the loan you are requesting is reasonable.

The financial forecast should include a balance sheet

and an income and cash-flow statement. The balance sheet is a statement of what the business owns and owes; the difference is referred to as "net worth." An income and cash-flow statement shows when the money comes in, indicating whether it flows seasonally, or depends upon holiday sales, for example. It also indicates the difference, when all cash payments and cash income has been accounted for.

8. *Appendices.* A copy of the franchise agreement, along with any lease or sub-leasing agreements should be included to give the bank a full picture. For example, if you are asking for a five-year loan and leasing premises that have only three years left on the lease, the bank will certainly want to know how you intend to conduct your business after the lease expires. If you are forced to move, for example, how much will relocation costs be? How much money will you have to spend on new in-store promotional activities, stationery, packaging identification and advertising?

Hertzberg's final advice to prospective franchisees on their way to make a presentation to the bank is to look the part of a business person. "There is a rather famous story circulating around the franchise community of the young man who prepared the best information package that the banker could ever have wanted," says Hertzberg. "Unfortunately the banker never even read the material.

"The franchisee, who was going to open a store selling T-shirts, walked into the bank wearing a sample of his products to show the banker. Now, T-shirts are not the best apparel to wear when meeting a prospective banker, but this one had a picture of a great big turd on the front and some unsavory comments underneath the picture. The loan was not granted."

Hertzberg's sample loan presentation and business plan include a worksheet to assist you in calculating your net worth and the total projected investment of the franchise:

TOTAL PROJECTED INVESTMENT COST OF A FRANCHISE – A CHECKLIST*

*Total
Cost*

Initial franchise fee $ _________

Leasehold improvements (alterations to leased premises)   _________

Development/design fees   _________

Furniture, fixtures and equipment–include taxes, freight
   and installation charges   _________

Signage–including production and installation   _________

Automobiles–including alterations, signage, licenses   _________

Deposits, permits, last month's rent, cash funds   _________

Insurance premiums   _________

Telephone installation, yellow pages   _________

Initial inventory–including supplies   _________

Training costs–including travel and accommodations   _________

Pre-opening costs–rent, staff salaries, utilities, supplies,
   wastage   _________

Site start-up, special staff   _________

Opening promotional campaign   _________

Initial bookkeeping supplies/services, stationery, invoices
   and business cards   _________

Incorporation costs   _________

Financing costs   _________

Working capital   _________

Franchise investigation costs:
   Legal–review of contracts/lease   _________

   Financial–cost/cash flow projections, bank loan
      applications   _________

   Market/site selection study   _________

Other costs (specify) ________________________   _________

                         ________________________   _________

                         ________________________   _________

TOTAL PROJECTED INVESTMENT COST $ _________

*Copyright 1988 by Price Waterhouse, Franchise Business Services

CALCULATION OF NET WORTH AND UNENCUMBERED CAPITAL – A WORKSHEET*

	Present Value	*Liquid Assets Available to Invest*
ASSETS		
Cash on hand and in banks	$ _______	$ _______
Government securities	_______	_______
Accounts, loans and notes receivable	_______	_______
Life insurance, cash surrender value	_______	_______
Other stocks and bonds	_______	_______
Real Estate–estimated market value	_______	_______
Automobiles registered in own name	_______	_______
R.R.S.P.		
Other Assets (specify) _______	_______	_______
_______	_______	_______
_______	_______	_______
_______	_______	_______
TOTALS	A $ _______	C $ _______

	Total Liabilities	*Short Term Payables*
LIABILITIES		
Notes payable to banks		
unsecured direct borrowing only	$ _______	$ _______
secured direct borrowing only	_______	_______
Loans payable to others	_______	_______
secured	_______	_______
unsecured	_______	_______
Loans against life insurance	_______	_______
Accounts payable	_______	_______
Interest payable	_______	_______
Taxes payable	_______	_______
Mortgage Payable on Real Estate	_______	_______
Brokers Margin Account	_______	_______
Credit Cards	_______	_______
Other Liabilities	_______	_______
TOTALS	B $ _______	D $ _______
NET WORTH/NET LIQUID ASSETS	(A-B) $ _______	(C-D) $ _______

ADD:

Mortgage financing available on house and
  other real estate up to maximum limits
    allowed by tender   E __________

Non-interest bearing loans from family,
  friends, relatives   F __________

UNENCUMBERED CAPITAL AVAILABLE FOR
  INVESTMENT IN FRANCHISED BUSINESS
  (C − D + E & F)   G $ __________

*Copyright © 1988 by Price Waterhouse, Franchise Business Services

Hertzberg suggests that you ask the banker if there are low-interest loans that are applicable to your business. The federal and provincial governments currently have special loans available for small business. The loan most frequently used in starting or expanding a franchise is the federal Small Business Loan (SBL).

The SBL provides guarantees to the lending institutions of 85 percent of the loan. These loans are available to Canadian startup businesses or to those with gross annual sales of less than $2 million. Although the loan amount is capped at $100,000, it is very popular with franchisees since its interest rate is set at 1 percent above the prime rate, the rate banks give to their best corporate customers. While your banker can give you the exact details of the SBL, the terms and conditions are essentially as follows:

• Your company must be in the manufacturing, construction, wholesale or retail trade; a communications business, real estate agency; or in the service-agency sector.

• The loan may be repaid over a term of up to 10 years.

• Funds can be used to finance up to 90 percent of the cost of land, construction of new premises, or in the case of leasehold improvements, the cost of renovation.

• Funds can be used to finance up to 80 percent of the cost of fixed or moveable equipment.

• The interest rate is set at the prime rate, plus 1 percent.

• The amount of the loan may be anything up to $100,000.

• There is a charge of 1 percent paid by the person taking the loan of the total amount of the original loan to help defray the government cost of the programme.

• The loan can be secured by a land or chattel mortgage or other asset.

• The granting of the loan is by no means automatic, but is at the discretion of the lender, who bases the decision primarily on your ability to repay.

7

Designated Products and Supplies

As a franchisee you may be required to purchase specific products or ingredients from suppliers designated by your franchisor. This only makes sense: the consistent quality of the ingredients in the case of a restaurant franchise, or the effectiveness of the technology in a service industry, may be the chief reason for your hoped-for success.

In the St-Hubert's chain, many of the ingredients are made by outside suppliers from whom franchisees are asked to purchase.

Mario Salvagna, who owns the Pickering, Ontario, franchise, says that he is required to purchase his baked desserts from a bakery designated by his franchisor. The reason is quite simple. Each St-Hubert's outlet features a brightly coloured wall poster illustrating the available desserts. Although Salvagna is free to add other desserts, his franchisor wants to be sure that the featured baked goods, an apple or sugar pie, for example, are identical in Toronto and Quebec City.

Salvagna says that he is considering putting in a yogurt-making machine, which will suit the economic make-up of his upwardly mobile, two-income, diet-conscious clientele. He would be free, however, to select the type of machine he wanted, and to purchase it from a supplier of his own choosing, since it would be an add-on to the St-Hubert's product line.

Sometimes franchisors introduce product lines, especially products the customer takes home, into franchise outlets in order to increase public awareness of the system.

This is the case with the Moneysworth & Best Shoe Repair system. According to franchisor Rick VanSant, the company produces an extensive line of shoe-repair and shoe-maintenance products, such as polish and shoe trees.

"We want the customer to take the product home almost as a form of advertising, so that they remember to come back to our outlets," says VanSant. All the Moneysworth & Best outlets are required to carry the house lines. However, they can also carry competing brands.

The same is true for the franchise outlets of First Choice Haircutters. In this case, the franchisor spent a lot of money to develop hair-care products that would be available exclusively to their franchisees if they chose to carry them. It turned out, however, that while most franchisees put the products onto their store shelves, they continued to use well-known brand-name products when working on clients' hair. Hence, the clients purchased the nationally known brands.

The hard fact was that First Choice did not have a national sales force able to compete with those of older, well-funded brand manufacturers. " 'We are a very new entry into the beauty supply market-place and our emphasis has been on cutting hair,' says Kostopoulos. 'Given these facts, sales of our products have been strong. We will be working in the future to set up a marketing programme that gives additional support to our product line and thus higher sales within our chain.' "

According to Toronto franchise lawyer John Sotos, having to buy products through the franchisor or the franchisor's designated suppliers can raise a few problems for the franchisee. The advice he offers to his clients includes the following points:

1. *Make sure the designated products will be priced competitively.* Volume rebates are regularly available to customers who can buy in bulk. Generally the rebate goes to the franchisor. Still, most reputable franchisors will warrant to the franchisee that the prices charged for mandatory products are better than, or equal to, the price charged for the product or service to non-franchisees.

If a franchisor tells you that the price of the mandatory products will be higher than that paid by a non-franchisee in an independent business, take a careful look at the overall franchise package. Some franchisees of one pizza chain have signed franchise agreements in which they agree that the price will be no more than 15 percent higher than the current market price. The question in the franchisee's mind should be whether the franchisor gives such great advertising, service and back-up that the higher price for the product is worth it.

In another franchise system, a franchisee was required to purchase all its dairy products from a dairy designated by the franchisor. In the dairy industry, pricing is heavily influenced by discounts. This franchisor was not passing on the full rebates to his franchisees. For example, where the normal discount for a particular volume was 25 percent, the franchisees were only getting about a 5 percent rebate. The franchisees were assured a rebate; however, it was not a full rebate.

2. *Depending on the industry, watch for warranty history.* In the after-car purchase market–for example, mufflers, radiators and oil-and-lube jobs–be sure the franchisor is responsible for enforcing warranty programmes system-wide. As a franchisee, you don't want to have to enforce warranties on supplies chosen by other franchisees.

In retail merchandising, the franchisor should agree to warrant availability and supply. This is especially true in operations that have a catalogue. While larger organizations, such as Canadian Tire or Consumers Distributing, are better positioned to ensure a high level of supply, particularly on advertised items, smaller corporate chains might at times find that it is difficult to source product.

If the franchisee is located in a remote area, such as northern Saskatchewan, and the franchisor or the designated supplier is in central Ontario, for example, it is unlikely that there will be regional distribution. If such is the case, insist on written performance requirements of frequency of supply. Also, ensure in writing that the prices to you will not be higher because of your relatively remote location.

Other problems can arise when the franchisor is geographically removed from the potential franchisee. In a service franchise, for example, such as financial services or insurance, make sure that the services you are licensed to market are legal in the Canadian federal or provincial context. One U.S. financial-services franchise, whose principal business consisted of the sale of mutual funds, did not have the necessary licence to do business in Canada.

It would seem that under Canada's free trade agreement with the United States, duties, customs delays and price mark-ups could be minimized and American franchisors could easily move into Canada. It's unlikely, however, that we will see an immediate rush of American franchisors coming into Canada to compete with the existing systems. What is more likely is a gradual, but continuous, advancement into Canada of American chains.

While there are large American franchise systems currently in Canada, such as McDonald's and Kwik-Kopy, the real change will come in the field of small franchise chains. In the past, a small American franchisor who has outlets in Buffalo, New York, for example, and advertises on local television there has tried to set up outlets in Canadian cities that also receive the television signal. After all, why not get more for your advertising buck?

However, one of his biggest obstacles has been in sourcing product from the United States. Especially in contentious sectors in which Canada and the United States have held continuous trade battles, such as paper products (napkins imprinted with the franchisor's logo), there have been hold-ups at Canada Customs. Since the franchisor had only a few Canadian outlets, it didn't make sense for him to set up a full-fledged domestic distribution system and manufacturing facilities here.

Duties and tariffs have played havoc with the franchisor's cost structure. However, with the advent of free trade, over the next 10 years there will be a gradual phase-out of existing duties. They will still need franchise documentation and accounting practices to suit Canadian requirements, but these costs will be built into the franchise fees that are received by franchisors. When the advantages in the form of the devalued dollar and lower labour costs in Canada are added into the equation, eventually American franchisors might decide to set up manufacturing and processing facilities in Canada from which to supply their outlets, both in Canada and south of the border.

Another inducement, especially for small franchisors, to enter the Canadian market is the absence (except in Alberta) of disclosure documents. In contrast, in the United States each state has its own regulatory requirements and documents, and it can cost close to $15,000 (U.S.) just in legal fees to set up shop in each state. This is expensive enough that Canadian franchisors seeking to expand south of the border, unless they are mature and established and have solid financial backing, may decide to tackle the large American markets that are adjacent to their home province, test out the concept in the American market and then proceed cautiously into other states.

For the small Canadian franchisor, the reality is that until trade mark, disclosure and registration requirements in the United States are standardized, the paperwork trail will prove prohibitively cumbersome and time-consuming.

8

Affordable Franchises

Restaurants and retail operations are the most visible franchises since they generally have storefronts or factory-style outlets where the public comes to buy the product. They are also the most expensive to purchase–a St-Hubert's can cost the franchisee a total investment of $900,000. A retail franchise, such as Signor Angelo, while not in the same league as some of the fast-food outlets, can still command a total investment in the range of $200,000.

Investments of this magnitude are well above the limit that most franchisees can finance, even through a combination of personal assets and loans. That is one of the reasons that many franchisees are turning to the service sector, where franchise operations, some with total investments as low as $20,000, are still relatively affordable.

These are often "mobile businesses" that operate by sending out work teams in a truck or car. The advantage of such a business is that the franchisee can expand by adding two or even three teams, as customer growth warrants. Since many franchisees can make a profit of $25,000 to $30,000 a year per mobile unit, the goal is to run as many units as possible while still providing good service, according to Bob

McCannell, former national sales and marketing director of Turf Management Systems Ltd., the company that franchises the highly successful 95-unit Weedman chain.

One of the reasons that these franchises are inexpensive is that they can often be operated from an office in the owner's home. The franchisee generates leads and sales by direct mail, and telephone and door-to-door canvassing. A technique often employed is to hire teenagers to make "cold calls" to potential clients. Or, in the case of Photo-Pet, the franchise that takes photos of client's pets in their homes, franchisees leave fill-in cards offering one free photo in the offices of local veterinarians and at open-air markets.

Service franchises often develop a successful formula by rejuvenating industries that, for one reason or another, have an unattractive image. A careful and comprehensive marketing plan, involving, for example, painting the franchise's vehicles in the same colours, and dressing the franchisee and staff in smart uniforms, creates a whole new public perception.

According to Bob McCannell, the key to developing a clean corporate image in any industry that is widely regarded as ill-organized is specialization.

At Weedman, customers are charged a once-a-year fee in the range of $150 and the company comes back several times during the spring, summer and fall months to spray the lawn. Franchisees do not plant flowerbeds, rake leaves or trim trees, says McCannell. Therefore, Weedman franchisees become known as experts in one specific field.

McCannell is currently employed as the marketing director for Franchise Horizons Ltd., a firm that works with franchisors in the development, marketing and recruiting of franchisees. He specializes in the service franchise business. On behalf of a new client, Action Duct Cleaning Ltd., which has seven franchisees, McCannell is aiming to bring the same responsibility to the duct-cleaning industry that Weedman brought to the tending of the nation's lawns.

"Duct cleaning now is viewed exactly like weeding was in

the early 1970s," says McCannell. "There is an air of mystery about it. People want to know what they are paying for and why it is necessary."

Like Weedman, Action Duct Cleaning has decided to specialize. The franchisees don't do chimney-sweeping or furnace-cleaning or any other related services, according to McCannell. The only other service they will perform is, at the customer's request, to perhaps install an air cleaner.

Much of the service-based franchise market is made up of two-income working couples who haven't the time to spend on home maintenance that an earlier generation had. More and more franchises are springing up to meet the demand created by this market.

Many of these franchises look very attractive to prospective franchisees, says McCannell, because the costs of becoming a franchisee are so low. Action Duct Cleaning requires an upfront investment of $22,000. This includes a $15,000 licence fee that pays for the use of the trade mark and for training and business methods, and $7,000 for the initial launch, which involves brochures, work orders, office supplies, uniforms and window signs. There is also the cost of the Duct Vac 7000 machine ($21,000) and an automobile ($22,000) that the company suggests its franchisees lease.

Meanwhile, in national newspapers across the country, service franchises are being offered for as little as $2,500. These low upfront fees worry McCannell.

"Deciding to purchase a franchised service business because it is affordable, and because you want to be your own boss makes sense," he says. But where do you draw the line between, on the one hand, a business that is affordable and, on the other, a proven system with the support and backup that make a franchise worthwhile?

In order to assure themselves of the legitimacy of the business, prospective franchisees should find out if the flagship operation has been around for at least one full business cycle. If the company is brand new, there is no way a franchisee can know if the service being offered is one that the public perceives as necessary or desirable.

Another point to look for in an industry such as this is the frequency with which you can expect clients to require the performance of the service. Duct-cleaning, for example, is a three- to five-year repeat business, so the franchisee's territory has to be large enough for the franchisee to keep busy before established clients call for repeat visits.

Prospective franchisees of service businesses sometimes buy the franchises because they are seasonal, presumably hoping to lead an easier life. But, according to McCannell, franchisees are still putting in the 2,000 or 2,500 hours per year that they would be in a year-round business. In the case of Weedman, which is weather-related, 12 months' worth of income has to be earned in 8 or 9 lawn-growing months.

The same is true of any service business that offers reliability as one of its selling points. Seasonal or not, when the job is required, the franchisee has to be there to perform it. The franchisee bears exactly the same responsibility as the owner of a retail outlet who is bound to ensure that the doors of his or her store are open every morning at the same time.

9

Branchising

Ron Chappell knows that, as the first franchisee in the Agnew Shoes store-franchise system, his performance will in many ways determine the direction of the growth of the system. This situation would not ordinarily be an unusual one, except that Ron has worked for the Agnew chain for the past 28 years.

After 111 years in business, the Agnew Group Inc., based in Waterloo, Ontario, decided to slowly begin to franchise some of its 353 company-owned outlets. Five outlets have been franchised and Agnew hopes to have 50 franchised by 1990 as the programme gets rolling.

In the words of Ross McCallum, the partner at Price Waterhouse who is assisting the Agnew Group to make the transition, Agnew's move is part of a trend to "branchise."

"Branchising is simply defined as taking company stores and turning them into franchise outlets," says McCallum. "This is an especially attractive option for retail companies who are looking for hands-on owner-management to increase profitability."

Agnew Group president and CEO Bill Janci says that franchising is a natural business method for companies such as his, which are in the retail business. "The driving force in our decision to franchise our outlets was the increasingly competitive nature of the retail business," says Janci. "We already had a lot of leverage in terms of securing our locations since we are a major player in the retail industry. Our products and their lines of supply were in great shape. But what we didn't have was the people to make the corporate stores tick.

"Every retailer in the country has signs up advertising for retail help and we were no exception. However we knew that in franchising our stores we would be getting owner-managers who would provide stability to an outlet as well as work longer hours [because they would] have a personal equity in the business."

For prospective franchisees, branchising offers a chance to become part of an operation that is usually profitable, but at the very least is up and running. In fact, for employees of large-scale corporate retail operations who are considering branchising, or for people with extensive retail experience, branchising constitutes a completely new opportunity to own a business. Two of Agnew's five branchised units were purchased by company personnel from the stores. Of the 50 projected branchises this year, Janci estimates that only 20 percent will come from the ranks of store managers or head-office personnel. Hence, there is plenty of room for outsiders.

Most firms that decide to branchise take at least several years to complete the change-over and they frequently retain some company-owned stores.

At Agnew, for example, Janci says that plans call for 35 to 40 of the stores to remain company-owned, two or three in each major urban centre. This fulfils the company's promise to the franchisees that they will continue to have an equity interest, and therefore a stake, in the franchise system. It will also provide a proving-ground for potential new management people coming from the corporate stores into head office to fill the marketing, merchandising, buying and operational positions.

"We also have to ensure that we set the tone for the entire chain by keeping our fingers on the pulse of what is happening in the market-place. . . . That means being out there on the front line, which is the retail store," adds Janci.

Currently the Agnew Group's stores are divided among three concepts and store names. The Agnew chain of family footwear stores ("from the day you are born onward") is comprised of 243 outlets. Aggies, with 78 outlets, sells mid-priced, trendier shoes to the 18 to 30-year-old market. The Ashton chain, with 32 stores, is targeted toward a higher-end, all-leather product market. Of the five stores that Agnew Group has branchised since the autumn of 1987, all are in the Agnew Group. Aggie's will soon be branchised, says Janci. However, the two-year-old Ashton concept is still being tested while the company finds its market niche. It's not yet ready to be formatted into a branchisable business system, according to Janci.

The move to branchising cost Agnew over $100,000 and had to be undertaken circumspectly. Janci explains: "We had to answer questions from our store managers as to how they might continue to develop and grow. Then we had to reassure them that this will be a gradual roll-out process. Once they didn't feel threatened many of them started to think about purchasing a unit themselves."

But some managers simply don't want to own a business, says Janci. Others cannot come up with the necessary funds. An Agnew franchisee pays $30,000 in upfront franchise fees. A further $170,000 is required, split evenly between inventory and fixed assets such as leasehold improvements, shelving and signage. There is also a 2 percent advertising and a 6 percent royalty fee.

And other managers don't like the change to a franchising concept. Janci says the company produced videos on branchising, which were sent to district managers to show to and discuss with their regional individual store managers. "We are dealing with culture shock here, along with an element of fear of the unknown."

At Agnew, a lot of pressure is being felt by new branchisee Chappell, who says that he is a test case, a good "guinea pig" for the system.

"Traditionally a retail store has a new manager every six months or year as managers get transferred, especially as they move up the corporate ladder to bigger and bigger stores," says Chappell. "But when you have put yourself in debt and become an owner, you're staying put."

Chappell is working his 1,300-square-foot unit in the Argyle Mall, in London, Ontario, with his wife. "We do hire part-time casual sales staff, but we try to work the longer hours ourselves," says Chappell. "After all, we want to keep the money coming back to the same pocket."

But Janci says that the company will consider the branchising of only those outlets that have the potential to return a profit to the franchisee within a reasonable time period. "I think a five-year payback period will make an attractive investment for our franchisees," says Janci. Further, he is predicting that the costs of doing business will drop 5 to 10 percent in the franchised outlets, as a result of lower salary costs and tighter stock control.

Janci admits that branchising will free up company capital for further acquisitions. "Footwear is not a technologically driven product," he says. "You have to be big to have clout. By expanding we can offer a higher level of service and product choice to our franchisees and the opportunity to expand the number of their franchised outlets within our chains."

An example of a more mature branchise system is The Angelo Corporation, the company that runs the Signor Angelo and Madame Angelo franchise system, an eight-year-old retail chain specializing in men's and women's accessories.

The chain is the brain-child of company president Amin Jivraj, who calls himself a born entrepreneur. In the 16 months between summer 1987 and November 1988, Jivraj branchised all 61 of his company-owned retail outlets.

The reason for the move to convert the stores, which together have annual sales of approximately $30 million, was not based on immediate economic plans for acquisitions or a need to reduce the flow of funds from head office. "We had more cash than we needed and a lot of bigger chains approaching us to buy us out, or at least create some sort of partnership with us," says Jivraj. "Our sole reason was service to our customer base."

Jivraj says that his merchandise makes his stores pretty recession-proof. After all, he reasons, a bad economy or even a slow-down in economic activity may lessen the chance of a man purchasing high-end suits or a woman expanding her wardrobe. But an accessories-only store carrying mid-range priced European items such as belts, shirts, sweaters and ties can always anticipate a steady flow of traffic.

Having said that, Jivraj, a natural raconteur who loves to recount the joys of being your own boss and retailing, admits that the retail sector is one hard nut to crack. And even when you are doing well, it's a continual challenge to stay on top. "When you cut through all the marketing and the merchandise selection components of your business, the only way you can truly differentiate yourself in the market-place is [by] the quality of the customer service you offer."

This advice comes from a guy who once lent a customer the cuff-links from his own shirt. "When we first started the chain and had only a couple of outlets, I managed the Oakville, Ontario, outlet myself," says Jivraj. "One morning I opened the store to find a customer standing outside waiting for me to arrive. I can't tell you how thrilled I was to discover that we were so popular that people were lining up." He laughs.

As it turned out, the man had an important meeting and was so harried that he had left home without inserting his cuff-links. Jivraj took off his own cuff-links and lent them to him.

"Why should he have to pay all that money for a one-hour meeting?" asks Jivraj. "I felt that if I sold him the cuff-links, I was really taking advantage of the guy." Of course, says Jivraj, the man is now a regular customer.

As the chain grew, Jivraj says that the shortage of good retail help, and the challenge to his field managers to stay on top of each individual store, convinced him of the need to branchise.

In 1985, Jivraj branchised two stores and tested them for a year to make sure his concept was workable. Sales in the two stores rose an average of 20 percent with the hands-on management. Once he was sure the system would work, Jivraj says his decision to branchise took on steam and was completed in record time.

The decision to branchise meant that Jivraj himself went through a year of hell in the corporate head office. He promised his 250 employees nation-wide that not a single job would be lost. Still, in his head office a number of management people quit.

"Several key personnel could not make the transition and feel comfortable with their new roles," says Jivraj. "They didn't like the fact that the head-office customer was no longer the person who walked into our stores. The new customer was our franchisee. Some of the management staff felt that they would experience a real loss of power and as a consequence their egos were bruised."

At the store-manager level, there were also a number of angry employees. But as a result of attrition, staff transfers into the corporate head office, and the fact that almost 30 percent of the franchisees are ex-store managers, the situation has eased a good deal.

Each of his franchisees has to demonstrate a flair for retailing, says Jivraj. Whether it is a Madame Angelo or Signor Angelo outlet or an outlet combining both, the franchisee also has to have good problem-solving skills and be something of an entrepreneur. His owner-managers have to understand that they are franchisees, required to check with head office on many decisions, but once Jivraj has installed them in their turnkey outlet (the store is completely constructed, stocked and ready to open), the franchisee has to be able to react to crisis situations.

In Montreal's trendy Promenades de la Cathédrale on St. Catherine Street West, 28-year-old Serge Gauthier and a partner run a combined Signor Angelo/Madame Angelo outlet. Gauthier is the former manager of the First Canadian Place office-tower outlet in Toronto. He took advantage of the branchising decision to return to his native province.

Gauthier says that the decision to branchise meant the

chance of a lifetime for many young store managers. "How else could I have got into business so easily?" he asks.

"If I had gone to a bank and tried to open an independent business like this, they would have turned me down. But between my experience in the chain, and the backing of an already existing, up-and-operating franchise system, I could find the money I needed."

Signor Angelo/Madame Angelo franchisees pay a $25,000 franchise fee per outlet, and make a total investment of $200,000. There is an ongoing royalty fee of 8 percent. Since the chain does not advertise in newspapers or radio, preferring, as Jivraj puts it, to let the big players generate interest in the market-place and the malls, there is no advertising royalty.

Gauthier has run his outlet as a franchisee for several months. He anticipates that since no franchise system is perfect there will be minor problems to overcome. Of immediate concern is the lack of bilingual personnel in head office and the resulting lack of French-language store signage. He says that, as a result, unlike English-language stores in the chain, he has to create his own in-store advertising and headers and other promotional material. Gauthier says that this is a small bug in a system that is still being worked out. He has spoken to his franchisor and expects the French-language signs to be in the works soon.

Buying a Branchised Unit

Buying a branchised unit presents a different type of challenge to the franchisee, says John Sotos, a Toronto-based lawyer who specializes in franchising.

Sotos has represented 18 clients who have purchased Consumers Distributing stores, a nation-wide chain of catalogue shop-in-person or shop-by-phone outlets. He says that unlike franchisees in the Agnew Group and Signor Angelo chains, Consumers Distributing potential franchisees had no comparable franchise system to which they could refer.

Consumers' closest competitor is the Sears catalogue

in-store outlets, according to Sotos, and since Sears is not franchised, comparisons with it are not useful.

"I think we are going to see a trend over the next several years, in which industry retail specialty outlets and services are branchised in sectors that previously have only been company-run," says Sotos. "The prospective franchisee will therefore be much more on his own in terms of investigation."

Sotos says that, at present, store managers and head-office staff who are given the chance to own their own stores are often dangerously complacent. "Some of these potential franchisees walk straight into the franchise without even blinking an eye. They don't investigate. They simply take on blind faith that, since the corporation was good to them in a corporate role . . . it will be equally satisfying to be a franchisee in their system."

Sotos says there are some areas of particular concern in newly branchised systems. He recommends that prospective franchisees:

1. *Find out if the franchisor has the staff in place.* For the system to operate smoothly, there must be experienced people to deal with key functions, such as ordering, financial assistance and warehousing. If you purchase an outlet in a mature franchised system, there is already a management team there that knows how to deal with franchisees. Make sure that the team has a franchise and not strictly a corporate orientation.

2. *Find out whether the pro-forma statement reflects a corporate or franchised product price.* The pro-forma statement is a financial projection designed to predict the cost of goods. Historically, the costs rise when stores are branchised, to pay for servicing the franchisee. The difference between $1.50 and $1.75 on each item can make a huge difference to the bottom line.

3. *Make sure that the franchisor does not intend to expand into another trade mark that may be in competition with yours.* This can erode your market share. Whether a client buys a microwave from you or a carriage-trade store

several blocks away can affect your profitability. (A mature corporate system will likely refuse to build into your franchise agreement a guarantee that they will not open conflicting trade-mark outlets in your area. You can, however, ask for right of first refusal, and so have the opportunity to maintain or even increase your market share. Then, the decision is yours.)

4. *Check to see if your agreement requires you to buy discontinued or dated inventory from the franchisor.* A corporate chain turning to a franchise system may have a full warehouse of products to unload.

5. *Check that the franchisor's distribution system is designed for a franchised outlet.* Remember that a corporate chain works on the "push" system, as the buyers decide on merchandise selection and force feed products to their outlets. A franchise system, however, should work on the "pull" system, so that you as the franchisee decide what products you feel will sell in your particular store.

10

Single, Multiple and Area Franchises

Once a franchisor has several outlets in operation, a decision has to be made about the best method of further expansion. Cheryl Kostopoulos, franchise director of First Choice Haircutters, often leads seminars on the subject. According to Kostopoulos, different franchisors have different names for the alternatives that are available. One chain calls its multi-store franchisees "area developers," for example, while another franchisor labels his sub-franchisor an "area" or "master" franchisee, but they can all be reduced to three clear choices that can be mixed and matched: *single-unit* franchises, in which a single outlet is purchased; *multi-store* franchises, under which a franchisee has the right to develop a predetermined number of outlets in one geographical area; and *area* franchises (sometimes called master franchises), in which an area is sold to a single franchisee who then sub-franchises outlets.

These alternatives represent very distinct opportunities to the franchisee from the moment he or she buys into the system. Or, to put it another way, the choice made at the outset puts legally binding limits on the ability of the franchisee to grow. If, for example, a franchisee buys a single unit, and later wants to expand within an adjacent geographical area, the decision he or she made on joining the system is likely to restrict future actions.

The single-unit franchise: In this case, the franchisor sells each unit singly to an individual franchisee. A single franchisee generally owns no more than two or three units. This style of development does not allow for rapid growth, because the franchisor has to determine the suitability of each franchisee before he or she joins the system. In addition, a franchisee generally does not purchase a second or third unit until the first outlet has been running profitably for several years.

The multi-store franchise: In this second arrangement, the franchisor sells the right to develop a certain number of stores in a given geographical area within a set time-period to one franchisee. The franchisee has to come up with the money for the first couple of stores and then opens new stores with his or her profits. However, if the franchisee does not live up to the terms of the contract, including the specified number of outlets that must be opened and the schedule of openings, the franchisee loses the rights to that territory. The franchisee does, however, retain the ownership of the stores that have been developed.

The area or master franchise: A franchisee purchases the right to sell franchises in a particular area. The area franchisee shares with the franchisor the royalties that recruited franchisees pay into the system. Like the multi-unit franchisee, the area franchisee has to come up with enough money to buy the territory, which can run into the hundreds of thousands of dollars.

The single-unit franchise is the slowest method of growth, acknowledges John Johnson of Kwik-Kopy Printing Canada. However Kwik-Kopy, which is itself a master franchisee of an American company, sells each unit singly. "We want to have owner-operators who actually manage their individual stores," says Johnson.

While there are a number of franchisees who own more than one unit (but generally no more than three), Johnson says that most of his franchises are owned by more than one person. "I can count on the fingers of one hand the number of sole-proprietorships in our system," he says, noting that there are 103 franchisee-owned (no corporate-owned stores) in Canada. "We're looking for hands-on management."

Given that premise, Johnson says that having area franchisees, each with seven or eight outlets, doesn't fit his company's expansion plans. However, Johnson says, franchisees in his system can expand even if they only own a single unit within a specified territory.

"Let's say that a franchisee wants to serve clients in their own trade territory [but not in the immediate] neighbourhood and whose orders are not large enough to justify making deliveries. . . . The franchisee can still get their business by opening a satellite centre.

"This is really a press-less centre in which there are facilities for photocopying and bindery. For the big jobs that require printing, the franchisee takes the work back to the mother shop."

While a Kwik-Kopy franchisee initially pays a fee of $49,500 for a franchise, the smaller, press-less centre would cost only around $7,500. "The franchisee has already paid for the licence and received his training," says Johnson. "The cost in the satellite centre is developing the site."

Johnson says that the franchisee could conceivably make a larger profit from operating two outlets that each have annual sales of $500,000 than from one outlet with sales of $1 million. "The satellite store costs very little to run as it is not fully equipped and there is usually only one staff person," says Johnson. "There's potential for a higher profit margin in that store."

While franchisors repeat over and over that they want their franchisees to follow the rules of the system to maintain uniformity, often the franchisee can find novel ways of demonstrating entrepreneurial skill and expanding the business, ways that the franchisor will gladly accept.

Such initiative is clearly shown in the case of the shoes

that travel 200 miles, from Fort Frances to Thunder Bay, Ontario, to be repaired at one of Vince Stilla's Moneysworth & Best Shoe Repair franchises.

Franchisee Stilla was one of the first to join the Moneysworth & Best system when the corporate chain decided to expand by franchising in 1987. He says he wants to emulate in a small way the entrepreneurial zeal of company founder Rick VanSant. VanSant is the man who in 1982 hit upon the idea of offering a tie-narrowing service through dry cleaners and parlayed the idea through much of North America, ultimately altering some 250,000 ties.

VanSant, who is convinced that personal service is the wave of the future, researched the market and decided that the number-one personal service so far unexploited was definitely shoe repair. He founded Moneysworth & Best in 1985, franchising it two years later. By November 1988, he had 70 outlets (21 company-owned) with annual sales of $9 million.

Taking a page from VanSant's book, Stilla looked around Northern Ontario to find untapped shoe-repair markets. What he found were the towns of Fort Frances and Dryden, each with a drawing population of 30,000, and both lacking a local business dedicated solely to shoe repair. And so the travelling shoe show was set up.

A dry cleaner in each town fills the role of depot for Stilla's operation. Once a week the shoes that need repair are sent by United Parcel Service the 200 miles from each town to Thunder Bay.

Stilla guarantees, weather permitting, the return of the repaired shoes within seven days, which he says is far faster than any shoe-repair service previously offered in the town. "People here used to send their shoes in the other direction, to Winnipeg, and get service that took three or four weeks," he says. If business stays good for a year, Stilla will probably open a mini Moneysworth & Best outlet especially designed to be a part of a larger outlet, such as a dry-cleaning business. The head office is drawing up plans for smaller (currently, outlets are 250 to 350 square feet) outlets to service smaller centres.

Stilla's total investment in each of the outlets he currently runs is in the $140,000 range, including a $10,000 franchise fee. He expects the mini-depots to cost much less.

For Stilla franchising has opened the door to success. "I get all the benefit of a franchisor who has tested the waters for me, but I can also call upon my own resources to get ahead."

For franchisor VanSant, Stilla retains enough hands-on management to represent the owner/manager style of controlled growth the company envisions.

In contrast, Cheryl Kostopoulos, of First Choice Haircutters, says that her 117 franchised outlets (85 stores are company-owned) are owned by just 38 franchisees (some are owned by partners).

"We want to grow faster than by selling individual units, so we feel that selling to multi-store owners is a good middle ground," says Kostopoulos. Franchisees currently in the system range from new multi-store owners who are in the early stages of development and therefore have only one or two units, to more mature franchisees who have up to 18 stores.

"If we were to sell to a master franchisee who then sub-franchised, we'd be one step removed from our franchisees. We want to deal with our franchisees directly, without a middleman," says Kostopoulos. "Allowing someone to sub-franchise your outlets is fine if that someone is really good at running a franchise system, in which case the sub-franchisees are really happy. However, if there is a problem with the sub-franchisor, your individual unit franchisees tend to blame the [parent] franchisor. We believe that the selling of an entire territory to have units sub-franchised doesn't allow for enough interaction between franchisor and franchisee."

Since First Choice Haircutters' multi-store owners are first and foremost business people who are not expected to function as haircutters, they are able to operate a number of outlets successfully. First Choice requires its multi-store developers to be fully involved, and will not sell to limited partnerships or to silent investors.

Kostopoulos says that areas granted to a multi-store developer have to make both geographic and economic sense.

"Ten stores based in the Toronto West/Mississauga area would make sense. There would be no long-distance telephone or courier charges, no overnight-accommodation charges, and the franchisee can supervise the stores without having to hire an extra supervisory person," says Kostopoulos.

The franchisee's mandate is to motivate staff, supervise operations, advertise the business and control variable costs. There is very little time spent on inventory controls and selection in a service franchise, according to Kostopoulos.

In the case of First Choice, the franchise fees for individual units in a multi-store system decrease as the number of units increases. The area-development right costs $25,000; the first two stores, $15,000 apiece; and each store thereafter costs $10,000. The profile of a typical area is 10 stores at a cost of $135,000. The development pattern would typically include the opening of two outlets after signing the agreement, and the opening of a new outlet every four months thereafter.

Among franchisors who do not agree that multi-store franchising is the best way to go is Ken Kadonoff formerly of O'Toole's Roadhouse & Restaurants, based in Toronto. O'Toole's prefers to develop individual stores in some areas, while selling "area" franchises in locations that are fairly far away from the company's head office.

"We don't like to develop individual units any farther away than a tank of gas will take me. . . . It is too hard to run them by long-distance telephone and by having to fly out there every time there is a problem," says Kadonoff. The company came to this conclusion in 1985 after opening and then closing outlets in Edmonton, Calgary and Winnipeg.

Kadonoff says that the long distances were not the only reasons that the restaurants failed. He explains, for example, that the liquor laws in Alberta force segregation of the dining and bar areas, a restriction that does not play well with the O'Toole's concept. But if O'Toole's had run their units through a local area franchisee, perhaps a compromise solution could have been found. As it was, he says, it was impossible to service the outlets, deal with immediate problems and prepare for further growth by what virtually amounted to remote control.

As a consequence, when the company decided to franchise in the Maritime provinces, it sold the rights to develop the O'Toole's chain in New Brunswick, Nova Scotia, Prince Edward Island and Newfoundland to John Eveleigh.

In the past two years Eveleigh has opened his own outlet in Fredericton and sold three franchises in Moncton, Saint John and Halifax. He expects to have sold seven or eight outlets by the end of 1989. These will include four units to a restaurateur in Gander, Newfoundland, who already owns 14 bars in the province. Within three years Eveleigh hopes to have sold 15 franchises.

Eveleigh, who has been in the restaurant business for more than 20 years, feels that he can be of great help to his franchisees. Although he prefers not to disclose the purchase price for the right to be the area developer, Eveleigh says that the sale of four or five outlets will allow him to recoup his investment.

As area developer, Eveleigh shares equally in the 5 percent royalty, based on gross sales, that all O'Toole's franchisees pay. However, the 1.5 percent advertising royalty they pay in addition does not go to the head office in Ontario, but stays in the Maritimes, where Eveleigh uses it to purchase local advertising.

The Atlantic provinces, in common with Northern Ontario, are five years behind areas such as Toronto when it comes to changes in restaurant and other business developments, according to Eveleigh. Therefore, he reckons that he and his franchisees get all the benefit of learning from the weak and strong points of the Ontario-developed system.

"Eventually, O'Toole's as a roadhouse restaurant will have to make changes, to update its concept, as does any other business," says Eveleigh. "Our advantage here in the Maritimes is that while the Ontario stores may have to try 30 different changes to find the three changes that spell success, by the time these changes make their way down here we'll know which are the winning ones.

"We may not have developed the O'Toole's system as early as many of the areas of the country, but now that we have started, our number of outlets will increase rapidly. Part of the reason is that we will develop with all the history and learning of the other outlets at our disposal."

11

A New or Established Franchise?

Business pundits like to say that any business that lasts five years has a good crack at success. Statistically that may be true, but for the franchisees of Mother's, a franchised pizza chain, statistics were not much of a consolation. When Mother's went bankrupt in 1988, the public was surprised, but there had been troubles in the system for some time.

In fact, those who bought a Mother's franchise in the year prior to 1988 weren't doing their homework. If they had taken the trouble to check with the owners of existing franchises, they would have learned enough to stay away from a franchise in which the ownership of the system had changed several times over a three-year period, and in which there was clearly dissension among the franchisees themselves. There was also disagreement among the franchisors and franchisees in regard to subjects as diverse (but crucial) as menu and pricing.

In 1989, the Mother's system was purchased by Little Caesar International Inc., a well-known pizza chain franchisor with great depth of management. It is likely that the new owners will bring stability and growth to the system.

Yet, with occasional exceptions, it is generally safer to buy into an established franchise system. The problem, from the point of view of the prospective franchisee, is that the best-known, most attractive franchise systems are likely to be sold out, at least in the major urban areas. Since one of the attractions of a well-managed franchise system lies in its integrity in maintaining protected trading areas, the company is not going to let you into a piece of the action unless you are prepared to change cities or neighbourhoods. So, if you want a piece of the franchise pie without relocating you may have to consider new systems.

And here lies the dilemma. If you get in on the ground floor of what will ultimately be a successful system, you are going to do well financially. But if the system goes belly up, or has so few franchisees that the basic attractions of franchising—mass purchasing and advertising power, for example—never develop, then you have paid your fees and royalties only to find yourself no better off than if you had decided to open an independent business.

So, how can you tell, by reading the numerous advertisements in local and national newspapers, which franchises will be the ones prospective franchisees kick themselves for neglecting five years down the road? It's simple. You can't.

Not surprisingly, given the number of franchise systems for sale, some franchisors test the market, don't find suitable matches and go back to the drawing-board to draft a new game plan.

Such was the case with Flyaway Indoor Sky Diving, a fabulous concept for simulating the thrill of free-falling from an airplane using the propeller from a DC-3 airplane and a silo-shaped flight chamber. The franchisors—the inventors of the simulator—offered franchises for sale in the early 1980s.

However, according to Bill Punt, the franchisors had a couple of strikes against them when they first put the concept on the market. Punt is the management consultant who now works for the franchisors to establish the first Canadian franchisee. In the first place, he explains, the total investment required to open the franchise in 1983 was $400,000, a rather awesome figure for an unproven idea at a time when the country was just coming out of a recession. And second, they had no showcase outlet to show to prospective franchisees. They had only the one outlet, in their factory near Montreal, which has been in operation since 1979. Since the factory was outfitted as a factory-cum-research facility, it was not a good advertisement of the concept to prospective franchisees who wanted to see what the outlet would look like made up to attract customers.

Today, the required investment has risen to $600,000, but this is not out of line in the world of franchising. The franchisors have sold one franchise to a buyer in Nashville, Tennessee, and it is thriving today. In 1989, plans call for an outlet to be built near Cornwall, Ontario, and business-format plans have been drawn up. Two more potential deals are in the works.

According to Punt, the concept of Flyaway Indoor Sky Diving has always been sound. It was only a lack of understanding of what it takes to launch a franchise system that led to the slow take-off.

Stephen MacKneson, who with a partner is the franchisor of the new Sproll's Old Country Bread system, agrees that it is difficult to decide which new franchise to sink your money into. MacKneson has been in the franchising business for more than 20 years. He was the franchisor, until he sold his interest, of the well-known Buns Master chain.

Sproll's Old Country Bread is based on the 10-year-old Sproll's Fine German Bakery in Kitchener, Ontario, and its two-year-old sister operation in Cambridge, Ontario. MacKneson and his partner are looking for their first franchisee. He says that there are a lot of questions that interested franchisees should ask about any new system, including his own.

The first question is whether the principals of a new system have an equity interest in the operation. "The franchisor should own at least one or two company stores so that he has a real stake in the continuity of the system," says MacKneson. "If the franchisor tells you that his sole role is in selling units, my advice would be to run in the opposite direction."

MacKneson says that potential franchisees should also ask franchisors about their knowledge of that particular market sector. "You want to be sure in your own mind that the franchisor has enough background to know if the concept is feasible, let alone profitable. You also want to feel reassured that if, for example, there is research and development involved, the franchisor has the background and knowledge, or at least knows where to lay his hands on the information, to facilitate growth of the system."

After the initial questions are answered, ask for a full disclosure of the finances of their existing operations and, as with any franchise purchase, obtain the names of the principals and check with the Better Business Bureau, says Mac-Kneson. If the franchisor doesn't want to let you see what the bottom-line figures of the current operation are, then beware. Secrecy at the outset is not likely to become open communication later.

One way to decide if you are interested in a new concept is to compare it to a more established system in terms of what it offers, bearing in mind that the mature system might, for example, have such items as a newsletter that are needed to communicate with franchisees spread country-wide. (A newsletter would be helpful, but not necessary, in a smaller system.)

Does the new system have a procedural manual that shows daily operations? If so, ask the franchisor on what the manual was based, since the franchisor may have based it only on his or her own store. Ask to see what research has been done so that you will be able to determine if the manual reflects the specific needs of the operation or is simply a rehash and compilation of the manuals of existing systems obtained from former franchisees.

Check to see where the money is coming from to set up the system. Established systems have already worked out the bugs, and your money is therefore going strictly to site-selection, research and other items that will directly benefit you. Is the new system fishing around in the market-place with your money without sufficient financial backing or knowledge of the industry?

Ironically, in reality the franchisor is fishing with your money, although it may be ethical, well-intentioned fishing. The decision to buy a new franchise system is pretty much an act of faith in the ability of the franchisor to make a go of the system. Even after all avenues of investigation are exhausted, a new franchise system is less likely to succeed than a mature, established system. This means that prospective franchisees themselves must have the stomach to risk what could turn into a disappointing, and possibly financially disastrous, experience.

12

A Resale or New Franchise?

Jim MacKenzie, president of Molly Maid, a franchised home-cleaning service, never dreamt that the franchise system he designed to sell for $11,000 per franchise territory would have such a high resale value.

Molly Maid, an eight-year-old franchise system with 350 franchises world-wide (including the United Kingdom, the United States, the Scandinavian countries, France and Germany) with annual sales close to $40 million, is almost sold out in Canada.

Currently there are 165 franchises nation-wide, and the potential for only another 10 or 15 franchise territories. Since there are so few new franchises to be purchased, an active resale market has developed. This close-to-sold-out situation makes his franchises as valuable as gold. But MacKenzie doesn't want to hype the investment potential or tell tall tales of capital gains. "Like any franchisor, I anticipate there will be a turnover in franchise owners," says MacKenzie. "But I would hope that our turnover would not exceed its present level of 15 percent annually."

In 1988, a Molly Maid double franchise territory that had been worked for three to five years, and had cost the original franchisee $11,000 per franchise plus $2,000 to $3,000 working capital, was selling for approximately $100,000.

Other successful franchisors also play down the resale value of the outlets in their system, but acknowledge that the potential is there for a franchisee to work the franchise for a number of years and then make a good profit on its sale.

"Potential franchisees always want to know how well they can expect to fare if they decide to sell their franchise somewhere down the road," says John Johnson of Kwik-Kopy Canada. "In fact, they ask this question almost as often as they ask what they can reasonably expect to draw from the franchise yearly. Franchisees are sophisticated enough to know that the value in a good franchise lies also in its resale value."

In the Kwik-Copy system the typical franchise is a 1,500-square-foot outlet that, on average, would have annual sales in the $400,000 range. Johnson says that if a franchisee runs the outlet according to guidelines laid down by the franchisor, the potential exists for a 25 percent profit after all the costs of business, including long-term debt, royalties and staff (but not including the franchisee's salary).

A typical well-run franchise that is five years old (Kwik-Kopy has been franchising in Canada since 1978) would likely have paid off its long-term debt, says Johnson. The franchise could be resold for something in the range of $300,000. Taking into account the franchisee's original franchise fee of $49,500 and total investment of $120,000 to $150,000, the profit on selling the outlet is certainly reasonable. It is also usually easier to sell a franchised outlet than "Joe-Blow's" printing shop, according to Johnson.

Johnson says that Kwik-Kopy's turnover was almost nil until the chain hit the 100-franchise plateau. "We have a less than 8- to 10-percent attrition rate. But it is heartening to us that the franchisees who want to sell their units are generally healthy individuals who want to go on to new challenges."

Amin Jivraj, of the Signor Angelo/Madame Angelo retail chain, agrees that the resale market for successful franchise outlets is strong. Even though his franchise system is less than a year-and-a-half old, one of his earliest franchisees was offered $300,000 for the business. The franchisee had paid a $25,000 franchise fee and had made a total investment of $200,000, says Jivraj.

Franchisee Terry Hooey of Toronto bought into the Molly Maid system in 1987. She paid approximately $80,000 for her double franchise. The going rate is about $10,000 to $15,000 per cleaning team of two people, says Hooey. Most double franchise territories have seven or eight teams on the road.

Hooey says the business opportunity came to her as a result of her good luck and a friend's bad luck. Hooey, the former executive director of a school for the deaf in Toronto, had decided to look around for a business opportunity and visited several franchisors. Molly Maid was one of the franchise concepts that came within her financial means. Just as she was beginning to search for a Molly Maid franchise, her friend, then a franchise owner, told Hooey she was being forced to sell.

"Part of being a Molly Maid franchisee is leasing cars that your team driver uses both for work and as a perk of the job," says Hooey. "Unfortunately for this franchisee, one of her employees hit a pedestrian. Even though Molly Maid has negotiated group insurance rates for its franchisees, this franchisee's insurance fees rose so high as a result of the huge settlement that resulted from the accident that she couldn't afford to keep her team vehicles on the road. She had to sell."

Hooey says that she had considered starting a business on her own, but the high mortality rate for startup businesses put her off. She also investigated new franchise outlets in other franchise systems.

One of the most positive enticements for her to buy the Molly Maid franchise was that the groundwork had already been done. "I'm not sure I could have succeeded in this business if I had worked it from the ground up," says Hooey. "But in buying a resale I had the benefit of my friend having put all the mechanisms in place for a successful venture.

"If you buy a resale franchise, the customer base should be strong and, quite frankly, even if it isn't as strong as it should be, it's not as scary as tackling a new franchise business head on.

"People in the neighbourhood have grown used to seeing the blue cars with the pink decals, and the girls going into homes to clean wearing their navy blue French maid uniforms. When I bought the franchise, it was already a known entity."

Hooey says that although she will never get rich from owning a Molly Maid, she was able to draw a salary, pay her bills and be profitable from the word go. A typical Molly Maid double-territory franchise generates approximately $300,000 in annual sales. The women who clean on the seven routes bring in approximately $1,000 a week from their labours. The driver is paid about $300 per week and the helper $230. When all the costs of running the franchise are computed, including a 6 percent royalty and a 2 percent advertising-fund fee, leasing the cars and purchasing cleaning materials, Hooey figures she personally gets to keep about $35,000. Not a large salary, but she is certain that it's more than she would take home in the first year of a startup business.

Franchise lawyer John Sotos maintains the decision to purchase a resale unit or to start from scratch is by no means cut-and-dried. "There are a lot of factors to consider, the least of which is the amount of money you are able to invest in the business. You may find that you have to build your equity from increased sweat at the beginning of building up a franchise," says Sotos.

One of the most important points in considering a resale, however, lies in making sure that the existing unit is a current version of the corporate identity. If the corporate stores are on Image Five and you buy an Image Three, you will be asked within several years–or sooner–to pay for upgrading your outlet to the current market image.

Consumers Distributing, for example, which recently has

been branchising (taking corporate stores and turning them into franchised outlets), has updated over the past few years by adding jewellery counters to many of its stores. The costs of changing the image of a franchised outlet must generally be borne by the franchisee.

Similarly, Country Style Donuts, which traditionally had outlets of approximately 1,400 square feet, has recently changed the size of its units to 2,000 square feet in order to add soup, sandwiches and salads to its product lines. If you purchase an older unit, and there is physically room to expand, you may be asked, shortly after your purchase, to invest in new equipment and to renovate. If there is no room to expand, you will, unless it is specified in your franchise agreement, be paying advertising royalties that focus on the soup and salads, product items which will have no impact on your sales.

Sotos has prepared a chart outlining the differences between purchasing a resale and a new franchise.

MATTERS TO CONSIDER WHEN PURCHASING
NEW AND RESALE FRANCHISES

RESALE	NEW
Purchase Price: Higher than the Franchisor charges for new Franchises. Premium based on many factors including gross-income, term of lease and Franchise Agreement. Terms of repayment may be unfavourable; Bank Financing may not be available requiring the mortgaging of personal assets.	Relatively low. Favourable term of repayment often available through a Franchise Package (80% of leasehold and 70% of equipment costs).
Inventory: Must be paid for by cash on closing.	Usual trade terms.
Franchise Fee: No initial Franchise Fee as such.	Initial Franchise Fee which is not

	refundable. Amount may be up to $50,000.00.
Location: (a) Choice in location to be purchased. (b) Proven success of location.	Often no choice of location other than a geographic area. Unknown success of location.
Term: Something less than the maximum original term. Many Franchisors do not extend to Purchasers the maximum term for new Franchisees even if lease permits such a term.	Maximum term under Agreements.
Development of Franchised Location: No development costs or frustrations. If franchised business has been in operation for some years expect to renovate some time in the future. Most systems undergo a major renovation within 7-10 years. If Purchase Price did not take this factor into account, this expenditure will erode profitability.	If turnkey, relatively pain free. If Franchise must develop premises then multitude of frustrations and delays. New Franchisees should avoid developing site due to inexperience and the plethora of unforeseeable delays which may increase the cost of development.
Lease Payments: If Franchisor controls site or if located in major shopping centre expect to pay increased minimum rental upon resale. This increased rental continues even if business takes a downturn.	Generally as per original lease.
Royalties: Franchise Agreement may provide for increased royalties on resale.	Royalties usually fixed.
Advertising Contribution: Frequently increased.	Advertising Contribution more likely to remain fixed.

Form of Agreement:
May be required to execute new   N/A
form of Agreement which usually
is more onerous yet Purchase Price
paid may not reflect new term.

Exclusive Trading Area:
Often restricted on resale.   Greater opportunity to negotiate
                                   favourable territory but often
                                   restricted to the length of
                                   Franchisee's ownership of location.

13

Location

In the retail business format, location is of such critical importance that within a particular franchise system the franchises with the best ones can be two, three or even four times as profitable as those with an average location, according to Norman Rolfe of the Ontario Ministry of Industry, Trade and Technology.

As a result, franchisees who are all ready to purchase their franchise and start the building process can sometimes wait for up to a year before a suitable location is found for their outlet.

That was precisely the case with the Pickering, Ontario, outlet of St-Hubert's. Franchisee Mario Salvagna believes that franchisees should never underestimate the value of location. His actions underscore his words.

In fact, Salvagna felt so strongly about choosing the right location that he refused to compromise, even when he was in danger of losing a great deal of money, by settling for what he considered a lesser location.

When Salvagna signed his franchise agreement in September 1987, he could have chosen a site that would have been ready for construction almost immediately. After all, in the booming suburbia that Pickering has become, there are dozens of strip malls and free-standing buildings going up, apparently overnight. However, he had a specific site in mind: the end unit in a brand-new shopping centre located at the first business entrance to Pickering off busy Highway 401, which transports thousands of commuters into Toronto. The site can be seen from the highway, and drivers have easy access to the restaurant. Positioned where he wanted it, his restaurant could attract commuters going in and out of the metropolitan area.

But the mall was not due to begin construction until 1988. Then, in one of those cruel twists of fate, after construction began in the summer of 1988, strikes shut down the entire site. Salvagna, who still might have been able to get out of his lease, held firm, in spite of the fact that he had to ship his management people to a corporate-owned outlet and underwrite part of their salary just to keep them available for his eventual opening.

It was not until February 1989 that a proud, but relieved, Salvagna opened his restaurant's doors. At the time of writing the outlet has been open for two weeks, and there is a line-up in front of the restaurant every night–the line-up of hungry commuters that Salvagna had waited for so patiently.

On the other side of the coin, the scarcity of good locations was one of the reasons that the Dockside Restaurants, a seafood chain, failed to catch on, believes Ken Kadonoff, the chain's former chief executive officer. The Dockside Restaurants, run by the same group that franchises the successful O'Toole's, sold three franchises. Two failed and the third was absorbed into the O'Toole's system.

"For a seafood restaurant to be successful it has to be on well-travelled main arteries and there are very few of those sites available at a reasonable price," says Kadonoff. "If you look at the Red Lobster franchises, an already established American chain who were our direct competitors, they are on what we refer to as 'main drags.' "

In contrast, since the O'Toole's concept is of a local gathering spot, locations need not be those with high visibility and correspondingly high prices. The Dockside chain had neither the capital to be able to plug into the good locations, nor the financial backing to hang on until it could get the clout and money to negotiate good site deals, says Kadonoff.

Most franchise concepts do have fairly specific site criteria. Stedmans stores, for example, because they are located in small towns, have to be on sites right on or very close to the main street. A Flag Shop franchise (selling flags and related regalia) needs a location with a parking lot and access to a loading door.

Signor Angelo/Madame Angelo stores must be in a high-traffic area in a busy indoor mall. Ideally, says its franchisor, Amin Jivraj, the outlet should be within close proximity of a large department store, since the stores sell accessories.

"Mature franchisors have developed very precise guidelines as to where they want their locations," says Norman Rolfe. "Their expertise includes marketing specialists who study census, demographics and traffic patterns of specific locations."

One of the major reasons for purchasing a franchise, instead of opening an independent outlet, is that the franchisor is supposed to be especially good at selecting locations. But Rolfe warns that prospective franchisees should make sure to weigh the franchisor's recommendations against information obtained from existing franchisees. Ask them how their location works for them. Ask them what they would change, says Rolfe.

Rick VanSant, franchisor of Moneysworth & Best Shoe Repair says that location is so closely tied to profitability that it is the one component of his franchise setup in which no compromise is possible.

First, the franchise area has to have a population base of at least 50,000 people, says VanSant. (This criterion may change if the company decides to go with its proposed mini-store franchise.) So, while VanSant says the company has been offered a fabulous location in Dawson City, Yukon, which would have given his company representation in the far north, he reluctantly decided not to place a franchisee there.

Generally VanSant's decisions are based on whether a

particular mall has a suitable site. All but two of the system's 70 outlets, each of which is approximately 250 to 350 square feet in size, are located in indoor malls. The company's first location was in a 4,000-square-foot store on Toronto's busy Yonge Street near Eglinton. The location was not VanSant's first choice.

As the owners of the Dockside chain found, good locations can be hard to grab. However, because the Moneysworth concept needed only 250 to 300 square feet, VanSant could be audacious.

"I went to a number of malls and wanted to lease space, but all the developers wanted to see the store I was running already. So we leased a 4,000-square-foot space in a very visible storefront, carved 300 square feet out of it for our store, and sub-leased the rest. When we took the mall people to this outlet they were impressed and we were able to get all sorts of good locations thereafter."

Gordon Metcalfe, the founder of O'Toole's Roadhouse & Restaurants, agrees that first locations are hard to obtain. "When we wanted our first location, a site in Toronto, we approached a landlord near a major intersection in Scarborough. The landlord wanted to see our other restaurants and when we didn't have any to show him, he refused our offer. He said restaurants were an 'iffy' business." Metcalfe laughs in retrospect. "So many people said we were iffy, that I decided to take the company public by a reverse takeover into an old mining shell, and list ourselves on the over-the-counter market in Toronto. We didn't use the listing to raise funds, but to give us credibility. After we took this unusual step, landlords felt we were a known quantity and . . . we could get good locations."

Signor Angelo's Amin Jivraj also had difficulty securing that first location. "In 1980 we went to a major downtown Toronto mall and wanted to lease space. When the management asked for pictures of our other outlets, I showed them pictures that I had taken of some American stores, but in which I had left off the store name and logo. They rented us the space."

The recession hit less than a year after Jivraj opened his first store. Mall space country-wide soon became available as many retailers closed unprofitable stores or didn't take up options on upcoming space. Jivraj says that during the recession landlords were eager for his business, and he was given the choice locations. Jivraj, in turn, was eager to expand. His stores do well in a bad economy as people want to dress up their existing wardrobe.

Jivraj says that he doesn't tell the story to show how he hoodwinked the developer, but rather to demonstrate how hard it can be for a fledgling small-business person to gain a foothold.

The location of a franchise can alter the public's perception of the services offered, believes Moneysworth's VanSant. Shoe repair traditionally was off in no-man's-land in indoor malls. It was a clear case of out of sight, out of mind.

"Developers believed that shoe repair was a 'destination-service,' in other words, that people headed there anyway when they needed a shoe fixed or wanted to buy polish, [so] traditionally the shoe repair was in the 'Cinderella space' down by the furnace.

"The owners of the repair store, who were usually a Mom and Pop small operation, agreed to the location because it was inexpensive and they wanted the lowest-cost space.

"In contrast, we insist that we want lots of traffic flow and high visibility in our locations, so that people will see us and think of us the next time they need shoe repair done. We want them to remind themselves to bring that pair of shoes that need fixing the next time they come to the mall. We also want them to stop into the store to buy polish, shoe trees and other related items.

"As a result we refuse to take 'C' space. If the mall won't give us 'A' space, we won't take any space. We can't afford to take secondary locations."

Franchisees should go through the following list of factors, which has been adapted from a checklist supplied by the Ontario Ministry of Industry, Trade and Technology. The list begins with items such as the zoning and other physical aspects of the location and ends with the suitability of the demographics of the neighbourhood in relation to your product. Franchisees should be cautioned that a great overall location in a neighbourhood that is unsuitable for the product will have almost no chance of working. For example, locating a brand new Flyaway Indoor Sky Diving outlet in a neighbourhood chock full of retirement and nursing homes would be less than ideal.

1. *Zoning*. Is the current and future zoning compatible with your projected use? If it must be rezoned for your business needs, what time span is involved and what will it cost you?

2. *The Building*. Is the outside and inside appearance suitable at present for your business? If not, how much will it cost to renovate or decorate it to meet your needs? Does it make economic sense to renovate it to accommodate your needs when factors such as layout, lighting, heating, floors, acoustics, waste-disposal, parking, landscaping and snow-removal are considered?

3. *Transportation*. Does the location provide the access necessary for your business so that you can receive shipments easily and send them out quickly and economically? For example, are there shipping doors and truck access to the building? Are there any truck-road restrictions? Is there, for example, a ban on overnight parking that would prevent your leaving your vehicles or the vehicles of your suppliers in the parking lot? Is there a truck terminal nearby? Are there rail or air connections nearby? Is the location on a bus or subway route for your staff?

4. *Utilities*. Is there enough electrical power, water and gas to support your business? What would be required to upgrade them to meet your requirements?

5. *Taxes*. Can you afford both the current and future assessment for property and business taxes?

6. *Lease*. Has the lease been checked by your lawyer? Does it correspond to the length of your franchise

agreement? Are there any options available? Who pays to have the lease drawn up? Does the lease make clear what you are responsible for? Is it equally clear what the landlord is responsible for?

7. *Approvals*. Will all government regulatory bodies approve your use of the building? These include the fire marshall, as well as officials from the provincial ministries of health, transportation, environment and labour.

8. *Security*. Are there regular police patrols? Is there a fire station nearby? Are there fire hydrants to service the building? Is there a sprinkler system in the building? Is there a history of vandalism or break-ins at that location?

9. *Neighbourhood*. How stable is it? Is it getting better or worse? Is your business compatible with that of your neighbours? A muffler shop, for example, may not be welcome on the corner of a residential street. Would you enjoy living nearby?

10. *Restrictions*. Are there protective covenants that will limit your sales? That is, if neighbouring stores are selling certain types of product, will you be forbidden from carrying items that could compete with them? Is there room for your business to expand in size?

11. *Suppliers*. Are you near them? Is that important? Can you get quick service when a piece of equipment breaks down?

12. *Customers*. Who are they? What do the market-research studies (carried out either by your franchisor or by an independent consultant on your behalf) show about the neighbourhood's population in the categories of age, sex and income bracket? Are these demographics compatible with your business? Where do they live, play, shop? What would motivate them to buy *your* product? How often would they buy your product? Does the population fluctuate seasonally?

13. *Competition*. How big, old and strong are they? What percentage of the market do they have? What advantages do you have? (Your franchise's trade mark, for example,

or competitive pricing, may constitute advantages.) What advantages do they have? What percentage of the market can you reasonably hope to attract in that location?

Above all, says Rolfe, hold out for the right location. Don't let the franchisor push you into signing on the dotted line for a location you think isn't right. Remember Mario Salvagna. He's serving thousands of hungry diners who see his sign from the highway every night.

PART III

So You Want to Be a Franchisor?

14

Why Franchise Your Business?

In 1980 two Chatham, Ontario, brothers, Jim Tucker, a mechanical engineer, and Brian, an accountant, along with longtime friend, hairstylist Bud Cowan, decided to open a haircutting salon in London, Ontario. The threesome invested $150,000 in startup funds and opened the doors to their new venture, which they optimistically named "Superclips."

Based on a no-frills salon Jim had visited in California, the venture offered an "à la carte" styling service. A basic haircut cost six dollars, while add-ons, such as special shampoos, conditioners, a blow dry, hair colouring or perming, cost extra. Customers were able to choose the services they wanted on each trip to the salon.

In 1984, the hometown newspaper, the Chatham *Daily News*, proudly reported that the local trio was opening its hundredth store. Where? In Chatham itself. The company had expanded to 35 outlets throughout southwestern Ontario within one year of opening its first outlet in London. In addition, the newspaper reported, franchise agreements had been signed, with the result that new stores were up and running in areas as diverse as southwestern Ontario and Toronto, Vancouver Island, Alberta and Florida.

Since the appearance of the 1983 Chatham newspaper

story, Canada's largest franchised chain of hair salons has grown to consist of 85 company-owned outlets and 117 franchised outlets. According to Cheryl Kostopoulos, the company now owns 11 outlets in the United States, while franchised outlets number 41. The company projects that the total number of units up and operating in the United States and Canada will be over 750 by the end of the next five years.

The value of the operation's total international sales for the fiscal year ending in 1988 is approximately $30 million, with each outlet accounting for approximately $165,000 in annual sales.

Superclips changed its name to "First Choice Haircutters" in 1983 when the owners found they could not register the name as a trade mark in the United States, because of restrictions on the use of the word "super." By any name, it is a genuine Canadian success story.

In 1971, Dan Goliger, a commercial airline pilot, decided to change professions. He joined his father, Max Goliger, in the Montreal-based family travel agency, Holiday Travel.

Eight years later, father and son changed the travel agency name to "Goliger's Travel (International) Ltd." and moved the head office to Toronto. Although the original agency had already grown to include three additional agencies, the decision was taken to fuel further growth through franchising.

By 1987 Goliger's had grown to 60 franchises within Canada. The company boasts 1987 annual sales of $85 million.

Although there are more than 5,000 travel agencies in Canada, only 1,200 are part of a national franchise or corporate-owned chain. In franchising his system, Goliger says he is offering his franchisees a computer system that handles marketing and sales, outside sales representatives who account for over 20 percent of a franchisee's business, the know-how to operate in an industry that is regulated and most of all, national advertising and goodwill.

In August 1988, company president Dan Goliger

announced a restructuring of the company to accommodate the chain's plans for continued growth through both franchising and acquisition. Goliger's will henceforth be owned by H.W. Triumph Inc., a holding company owned by Dan Goliger; Lincoln Capital Corp., a Toronto-based merchant bank; and entrepreneur/franchisor *wunderkind* John Gillespie, former president of Pizza Pizza, Ltd., the Ontario and Quebec pizza franchise. Dan Goliger moves up to the position of chairman of the board.

The equity involvement of the new players was not disclosed, but Goliger's publicly states its intention to try to grow by another 140 units within five years.

Not every successful entrepreneur who decides to franchise his operation is going to enjoy the success of First Choice Haircutters or Goliger's. What works for some will not work for others. Before the owner of any business even considers expansion by franchising, there are a number of questions he or she must be able to answer satisfactorily.

"Just because an entrepreneur is doing well with one or two outlets, or a certain set of products, does not mean the operation is a likely candidate for franchising," says Dan Goliger. In fact, says Goliger, strait-jacketing an existing successful business by forcing it into a franchise mould can lead to the undoing of all the hard work and subsequent success the entrepreneur has achieved.

As a former chairman of the Canadian Franchise Association, Goliger often speaks to prospective franchisors. What follows is an expanded version of a series of questions Goliger has designed to help prospective franchisors ascertain if a business is franchisable.

1. *Is your business concept unique?* If something in the product, marketing concept or distribution isn't completely different from what is already available, then why would someone pay to be a part of the system?

2. *Will your product still be competitively priced?* This is a key question. The franchisee has to be able, for example,

to factor in a 5 to 10 percent royalty fee, a 2 to 5 percent national advertising fee, and a local 2 percent advertising fee and pay back the upfront franchise fee. In order to still sell competitively and make a profit, the franchisor has to be able to negotiate a volume purchase rate from suppliers low enough to accommodate all these add-on costs.

3. *Is your product proven? Does it have a successful record in the market-place?* Before prospective franchisees join your system, they have to be convinced that your product works. If it's a particular food, it has to be something that the public just loves to eat; if it's a device, it has to do what you say it will. Otherwise, you might be forced to sell the system for such a low fee that you will be unable to cover such costs as site location and research and development.

4. *Do you have adequate sources of supply for rapid expansion?* If the answer is no, be careful. Some franchisors make the mistake of saying that they will only open as many outlets as they can provision, only to fall under the spell of early successes and expand too quickly.

5. *Is your concept marketable nationally or only locally?* If the product is a regional food specialty, for example, consider either expanding the line (which involves delay for more research and development) or restricting the sale of your franchise to a particular region.

6. *Can your concept be kept uniform across the system or do you have to alter the concept drastically from region to region?* Remember, uniformity is the key to success. This holds true for such aspects as volume buying, but more particularly for advertising. Franchisees hate to pay for any advertising that is not actually promoting higher sales for them. One way around this is to sell area or master franchises (see Chapter 10) and then let the area franchisee run the system, adhering broadly to the overall concept, but adapting it to local conditions.

7. *Are there many locations suitable for your business concept? Can your concept succeed in a mediocre location?* If there are not enough suitable locations for the system,

give the thought of franchising a fast pass (see chapter 13).

8. *Are there enough suitable people available to act as franchisees for your system? Can your concept succeed with mediocre people as franchisees? Is your concept simple enough to enable you to train others to succeed?* A franchise system is only as strong as its franchisees.

9. *Do you have sufficient human resources to operate a franchise system?* In other words, do you have on board, or can you easily find and afford accountants, advertising managers, training staff and others to form the infrastructure necessary to support a network of franchisees?

10. *Do you have sufficient capital to run the franchise system until royalties from the franchisees start coming in?* Remember, the front-end fees are *not* the franchisor's profit! The franchisor's money comes from ongoing royalties. It may be several years before these are rolling in in sufficient amounts to make a reasonable profit for the franchisor. The front-end fees are part of the funds a franchisee pays for the right to use the trade mark, business format, and so on. This money should be used to promote the franchisee's chances of making it, by finding good locations and conducting research into new products, or by studying demographics, for example.

11. *Could the franchisee succeed only as part of your system? Would it be difficult or impossible for him or her to duplicate your concept independently?* If the answers are yes, okay. If not, watch out. We all know the story of the employee who walked out with the customers, suppliers and know-how to form his or her own business in competition with the boss's.

12. *Would the franchisee earn greater profits (after royalties) as part of your system than by going it alone?* If the answer is no, they why are you franchising? A franchisee who feels that he or she can do better as an independent is a dangerous franchisee. He or she may soon be spoiling for a fight (see Chapter 18.)

13. *Would you sell your franchise to your grandmother?* A franchise is only as good as the franchisor and franchisees who make up the system. If you aren't sure that it's good enough for Grandma, then perhaps you aren't sure enough to go ahead.

Dan Goliger's advice may be harsh, but it is even-handed. If all the component parts of a successful franchise aren't in place, consider making changes to your existing business before proceeding to franchising. Or forget about franchising altogether.

Some very successful businesses are not franchised, although as manager-operated chains they are so well known that the public probably thinks that they are.

Toronto-based Druxy's Inc., a 51-unit restaurant-delicatessen food chain with 1988 sales of approximately $40 million, is a case in point. Druxy's restaurants are concentrated in Toronto, with additional outlets in London, Peterborough and Ottawa.

Peter Druxerman, vice-president, marketing, says that the company receives approximately 40 to 50 telephone calls a year from people who think they would like to be franchisees. Many more people apply to the company to be store managers, hoping to become franchisees later if franchising is instituted.

"We are very truthful and tell people that although we have looked into franchising our concept, at this point we have decided to open only company-owned outlets," says Druxerman. "We simply feel that the reasons that would propel someone into becoming a franchisor are not compelling enough for us to consider adding franchisee-owned outlets.

"Companies franchise their operation for a number of reasons, including the need to raise capital for expansion," says Druxerman. "This is especially true if the franchisor wants to expand very quickly and take over the market-place."

Since its inception in 1976, Druxy's has worked hard to grow at a rate Druxerman feels is conducive to maintaining control. "Our feeling is that we would rather have a conservative growth rate and make sure that our concept is perfected in each of our stores than explode onto the market-place," says Druxerman.

"Our emphasis is on making our financial return from operating our stores. In franchising, a lot of the money the franchisor makes is from the front-end fees and an additional percentage from the royalties paid by the franchisees. But . . . it is hard to have a firm hand in each store since it is franchisee-owned, [and] it is equally difficult to be certain that the kind of operation you, as a business person, want to offer to your customers is really being maintained.

"We also feel that in a company-owned store you can train your managers and perhaps move them to locations that best suit their abilities. In a franchised operation, your franchisee is your franchisee. . . . [He] sinks or swims with the help you can give him, but you can't take drastic steps, if required, since the store is not company-owned. I guess what we are really talking about here is you as an entrepreneur controlling your own business."

Druxerman does not rule out the possibility of franchising in the future, particularly if the proposed franchisee is in a geographic location that might make company-owned restaurants difficult to control.

"Talk is cheap," says Druxerman. "If a guy walks into my office and wants to talk franchising and I really like him and think we might potentially make a deal, I'd say go ahead and talk. . . . I'm listening."

Karen Castelane is director of franchising at Woods Gordon, the management consulting arm of the public accounting firm Clarkson Gordon, a national accounting and consulting firm based in Toronto. Castelane often speaks to prospective franchisors. The following list of advantages and disadvantages of franchising is adapted from her analysis:

Advantages
- *Reduced capital investment.* Franchisors do not have to

plan for high capital investment in franchising. The franchisees' investment provides the necessary capital to facilitate overall system growth.

• *Expanded distribution and increased name awareness.* The proliferation of franchised units establishes a strong presence in the market-place quickly and very efficiently since there are many participants (that is, the franchisees), all working together toward the same goals. Rapid expansion enhances customer recognition of the trade mark, logo and, in some cases, easily identifiable buildings or storefronts.

• *Increased unit performance.* Having the manager-owner on the premises gives increased motivation and commitment and therefore improves store sales and customer service.

• *Additional profit centres.* Royalty and service fees from franchisees provide revenues in addition to wholesale profit margins. (The wholesale profit margin assumes that the franchisor either manufactures the products or makes a mark-up when selling the products to the franchisee.)

• *Ability to control overhead.* The responsibility for staffing and inventory management, which are frequently problem areas in rapidly growing organizations, is shifted to the franchisee.

• *Minimized risk.* Investment risk is spread between the franchisor and the franchisee.

Disadvantages

• *Reduced control.* Key areas such as pricing and merchandising may, in some cases, have to be left to the discretion of the franchisee because of local circumstances and legal restrictions.

• *Lower total profit.* Only a portion of retail profit in the form of royalty and service fees (in some cases in addition to wholesale profit margins) flows into the coffers of the franchisor.

• *Ongoing obligations.* Administrative and service support to the franchisees is required.

• *Legal and regulatory costs.* Paying for the franchise agreement and retaining legal counsel can be costly. If the franchisor decides to franchise in Alberta (the only province to demand that a prospectus and disclosure statements be registered), there are additional costs.

• *Inflexibility.* The franchise agreement sets the terms of relationship for a fixed period.

• *Risk of litigation.* Disputes may arise over numerous issues, including termination of the franchise relationship and the adequacy of support by the franchisor.

• *Risk of third-party liability.* The franchisor may be liable for acts or omissions of the franchisee.

After all the discussion, the decision to franchise may come down to four basic questions, says Castelane.

1. Do you have sufficient financing available, on terms that are acceptable, to fund your expansion as the corporate structure now stands?

2. Is your company's target rate for return on capital investment achievable through alternate expansion methods?

3. Will the system benefit from particularly rapid expansion?

4. Is it likely that the on-premises efforts of an owner/operator, in other words, the franchisee, would substantially improve unit performance?

"If the answer to the first question is no, while the answer to the last two is yes, then the entrepreneur should consider franchising the business," says Castelane. "At least at this point they should consider moving onto the next strategic planning stages."

15

How To Franchise Your Business

Few entrepreneurs, having decided that they want to franchise, are aware of the psychological change they will have to make, or of the adjustments that will be required in their overall strategic planning. For franchising demands a complete transformation: where once the strategy was designed to entice customers into a store or into using a service, in franchising the strategy becomes directed toward convincing the franchisee of the worth of the system and its products.

Another difference lies in the ongoing relationship of the franchisor and franchisee. An entrepreneur may have learned to deal with irate customers. They are part of the cost of doing business. As long as the number of irate or unhappy customers does not become so great that they sour the public's perception of a business, the entrepreneur may just have to accept the fact that sometimes a customer remains dissatisfied, for whatever reasons, and chooses not to patronize the business. Unhappy franchisees are less easily disposed of.

Like accounting procedures and product supply, franchisee management should be viewed as part of the overall strategic planning when contemplating a franchise system.

However, problems in strategic planning create the biggest stumbling-blocks in the way of new franchises, according to Ross McCallum and Jack Hertzberg of the franchise business services of Price Waterhouse, a national accounting and consulting firm.

A small business (usually defined as one with annual sales of up to $25 million) is not likely to have the staff in place to develop a franchise programme. Even if the company is medium-sized, with annual sales in the $25 million to $50 million range, it is still doubtful that they will have investigated franchising with sufficient thoroughness to have a programme ready to launch.

According to McCallum and Hertzberg, once the entrepreneur has made the assessment that his or her particular concept can be franchised, it is time to develop and fine-tune the various components of the franchise programme.

"The first stage of the process begins with strategic planning and flows through to offering continuing services to the franchisees once the franchise system is up and running," says McCallum. "A lot of entrepreneurs don't realize how many changes they may have to make, and how much staff they might have to bring on board, to facilitate expansion through franchising."

"The business owner has to plan just as thoroughly as he would if undertaking a corporate expansion. However, with franchising, provision also has to be made for making sure that a system is put in place that will allow the original business to remain viable and profitable.

"You don't want to neglect your business while you study all the implications of franchising," says McCallum. "One of the attractions to a potential franchisee in the first place lies in the strength and continuity of the store or stores in the current franchisor operation."

Price Waterhouse has developed a critical path for potential franchisors, which is outlined below in an expanded format. Although some entrepreneurs decide not to franchise after reviewing and evaluating the effect franchising will have on their operations, it is obviously better for both the franchisor and the potential franchisee if the entrepreneur backs away from the concept at this juncture rather than embarking on a business endeavour he or she is ill-equipped to handle.

A Critical Path for Franchisors
1. Financial Planning
First, the franchisor must determine whether the franchise concept is feasible. Presumably, the franchisor has conducted a market analysis for both the concept and the product and has included a study of the uniqueness of the product in the market-place and whether the product is seasonal (this affects cash flow).

The first task, therefore, is to develop a full-blown set of capital/earning/cash-flow projections for the franchisor and franchisee. One way to handle this is to begin by figuring out the rock-bottom price of the product and then adding on every little cost. While this procedure may not at first seem very different from financial planning for any corporate outlet, there are costs borne only by a franchise system.

Let's say that the product is a brand-new dessert product that comes in a wide variety of shapes and flavours. Now, if that product were marketed through corporate-owned convenience stores, the cost of the product might be $1.75. (This figure takes into account bulk-buying pricing, given the great number of stores.) But, if the stores are franchised and the cost is still $1.75, the franchisee has to account for, perhaps, a monthly royalty fee, based on gross sales, of 6 percent (10.5 cents); a monthly royalty of 2 percent for national advertising (3.5 cents); a local advertising fee of 1 percent (1.75 cents) and repayment of the front-end fee, let's say of $20,000.

Of course, the franchisee has to consider other costs that are pretty constant whether the business is a franchise or not, such as the construction of the building or payment of the lease, working capital and loan repayment.

The franchisor has to work out these costs to the franchisee to determine if the franchisee will still be able to compete effectively in the market-place.

Then, the franchisor has to take a hard look at the

potential royalties that will accrue, based on the gross sales of the franchisee, and determine if that amount will be sufficient for the franchisor to hire the support staff in key areas such as accounting, sourcing of materials and product, and advertising. More to the point, given the realities of the market-place, the franchisor has to allow time for the product to take the public's fancy, and make sure that the cash-flow projections show enough money coming in to keep the system afloat until higher royalties come on-stream.

One decision that the franchisor has to make at this point will influence the projections: namely, how the system will expand, as this affects cash flow and royalties (see Chapter 10).

The franchisor can sell single-unit franchises, in which case he gets up-front fees and royalties on a one-on-one basis from individual franchisees, or multi-store franchises to one franchisee, in which case the franchisee opens a certain predesignated number of outlets in a geographical area in a predetermined time-frame, thus ensuring the franchisor continuous growth.

The fastest method of growth, which gives the franchisor a lot of cash to work with, is achieved by selling area or master franchises. The franchisee pays a lump sum for the right to develop a large geographical area and to sell sub-franchises. The franchisor has to remember, however, that later on down the line the ongoing monthly royalties are split, usually 50/50, between the area franchisee and the franchisor.

Usually additional financing is required for both franchisor and franchisee, in the form of bank loans. Projections at this stage should include a realistic assessment of whether this financing is available, given the financial history of both the franchisor and the product.

If all seems sound at this point, the franchisor should approach a lending institution to try to arrange the appropriate financing. The worst-case scenario has the would-be franchisor hiring staff, lining up franchisees and then finding out that the bank is refusing to deal. Unhappily, some franchisors are so in love with the concept of franchising that they cannot believe they can fail. Bankers, however, have seen their share of franchise systems go belly up.

The third component of planning is franchisee recruitment and selection. This important part of the franchise process is dealt with separately, in Chapter 17.

2. Marketing and Sales Support

Since the trade mark and/or logo is what identifies the franchise to the public, the franchisor has to have a well-tuned advertising programme to build market identification.

The franchisor has to realize right from the start that the franchisees will want to be involved in deciding how their advertising contributions are spent. Therefore plans should be made for the establishment of a franchisee representative advertising committee. Working hand in hand with this committee, the franchisor must determine the kind of national, regional and local advertising dollars that will have to be spent to achieve the desired sales figures and growth in that particular market sector.

Since the system will likely have corporate-owned stores, it should be made clear at the outset what portion of this co-operative advertising budget is coming from franchisees and what portion from corporate head-office and corporate-owned stores.

3. The Operations Manual

The operations manual should be a comprehensive policy and procedures manual designed to make clear to all franchisees exactly how the system works and what they are expected to do on a daily basis. The manual should include such items as corporate philosophy, operating procedures, personnel policy, financial details, purchasing and distribution and merchandising.

4. Franchisee Training Programme

This area is one in which many new franchisors fall down. A franchisor who has run three or four corporate-owned outlets for a number of years may not realize just how difficult it is for a new franchisee to catch on to the system. In the restaurant business, for example, franchisees may not be aware that a detail as small as writing notes on the back of a napkin instead of on scrap paper can cut into the bottom line. Similarly, franchisees may have trouble ascertaining what levels of inventory they need.

Therefore, a school-like training programme should be set up. Part of this programme might be held, for example, at the franchisor's office to give the training a formal atmosphere. Of course, once the franchise outlet is open, follow-up training and daily on-site support should continue for some time. In a restaurant such follow-up could continue for several weeks. In a service business, a shorter time may be required, since usually only a single procedure is being taught.

Before a training programme begins, decisions should be made as to what will be taught and by whom, the size of classes and the material or equipment required. A detailed training manual that includes pertinent information and refresher tests is often a useful adjunct.

5. *Site Selection*

Before a franchise opens, much money and time are spent on securing the proper site to suit the system. This aspect of the critical path is dealt with in detail in Chapter 13.

6. *Accounting and Control Package*

To keep the system uniform, a set of record-keeping procedures that all franchisees will use has to be developed. This is especially important because it is out of these records that royalties will be determined. If these systems are not set up properly at the start and are not clearly stated to be mandatory for the franchisee, then later payments could be disputed. It is imperative that the franchisee understand that the agreement calls for franchisee auditing, and that this is not an invasion of privacy on the part of the franchisor, but is a part of the ongoing record-keeping practice and will make sure that every franchisee plays and pays an appropriate part in the maintenance of the system.

Bearing in mind that the flow of royalty payments is the life-blood of the franchisor, a slow-down or hold-back of payments on the part of several franchisees could mean that the whole system runs out of cash.

Of real importance is the initial decision taken by the franchisor as to how frequently royalty payments will be made. Some franchisors insist on bi-weekly payments, but as this requires time-consuming reporting procedures for the franchisee, monthly or even bi-monthly payments are the more usual choice.

7. Monitoring Systems and Ongoing Support

Before the outlet or home office opens, the franchisor needs to prepare a pre-opening checklist. This list should include everything from making sure the franchisee has enough inventory and enough staff to handle what ideally will be a crush of interested customers to planning for such small items as having a cash float for giving change.

Even if a franchisor thinks that he or she has invested a lot of time in the preparation of the franchise up to this point, what actions are now taken to facilitate ongoing support will decide if the franchise system makes it in the competitive market-place.

There is absolutely no point in sending a franchisee reams of paper and having the franchisee attend class after class, prior to opening, if, once the doors are open for business, the franchisee is left to sink or swim, while the franchisor goes off to court another potential franchisee.

8. Monitoring Mechanisms

Part of the franchise concept is the monitoring that goes on to make sure that the franchisees conform to the system. This means, for example, making sure that the sauce poured over a food product tastes exactly the same in Regina as it does in Halifax. The franchisor will need to hire, and then train, district managers. The training should include all the information that a franchisee gets. However, the manager should also have leadership and training skills and be able to provide motivation and moral support. The franchisor may decide to bring in specialists to help train the district manager in these areas.

There should be a system of communication with head office that ensures long-range reporting and monitoring when the district manager is not in attendance. Inventory levels, for example, can be reported and maintained through computer data-bases.

9. *Franchisor and Franchisee Communications*

Franchisees often complain that they are being inundated with systems bulletins, letters of direction, and newsletters. Some franchisors may go overboard, but if there is a change, for example, in the colour of napkins, or if a shortage develops of printed circuits needed to manufacture an electronic component, it really is the role of head office to inform the franchisee immediately. If head office isn't looking out for the franchisee, who is? Of course, the franchisor should appoint one or two staff people to co-ordinate the production and flow of paper, and make them accountable for the frequency of mailings. The cost of postage is high, and franchisees have the right to expect that two flyers be included in one envelope rather than being mailed separately two days apart. The royalties that go to the franchisor to handle these aspects are, after all, paid by the franchisee.

Still, after all the preparation, franchisors will forget problem areas or misforecast projections. McCallum and Hertzberg stress that individual franchise systems require varying amounts of pre-launch planning. Yet they insist that the franchisor who stints on initial planning will be constantly running circles trying to take up the slack later. Franchisees, they maintain, are demanding: they have a stake in the business and are impatient with franchisors who, in their view, act in a less than competitive or business-like manner.

Profile of a Small-Business Entrepreneur-Turned-Franchisor

Doreen Braverman never intended, when she purchased a regalia shop in Kitsilano, British Columbia, in 1975, that within 13 years she would be a franchisor.

Located in a fifth-floor, 500-square-foot office, the business sold traditional military regalia, such items as epaulets, gold-wire crests, braid and military buttons. Braverman noticed, however, that there was a steady demand for the small supply of pennants and flags she carried. Many of the people who purchased these flags were customers who came in for military paraphernalia. They might pick up one of her Canadian flags, for example, then ask if she could special-order provincial and marine flags. Some people even asked about personal and novelty flags and pennants.

"Customers kept asking for flags and banners and, although some of them were veterans, there were also a lot of younger homeowners, business people and collectors," says Braverman. "It seemed that no one business in particular was catering to this sector."

Sensing that a pent-up demand could be brought into the market-place, Braverman moved her outlet to a larger store-front location and renamed the business the Flag Shop.

At its first year-end, in 1976, the Flag Shop's sales had reached a modest $50,000, but at the rate the business was growing, Braverman believed she had scarcely scratched the surface of the demand. Along with flags and the hardware needed to fly them, she offered interior-design banners for retail outlets, decorator windsocks, party flag toothpicks and lapel pins.

Braverman was proved right. By 1981 she had expanded the business. Not only did she run the store in Kitsilano, but she had also opened Atlas Textile Ltd., a manufacturing business in the same city that specialized in flags and banners. With a partner she opened a Flag Shop store in Calgary. Annual sales for the two stores were close to $1 million.

Buoyed by success, Braverman decided to franchise the concept that year. "Unfortunately the recession hit with a vengeance," recalls Braverman. "The stores weathered the storm pretty well, but the manufacturing end really took a bruising."

It was not until 1987 that Braverman made the move into franchising. "My partner in Calgary had moved overseas, and with the one store and Atlas I felt I had enough to handle in terms of management," says Braverman. "In addition, I was also expanding Atlas. I really didn't have enough capital to take over the Calgary store and think about expanding into other retail outlets as well."

Braverman set the total investment for a new operation at approximately $75,000, including an initial franchise fee of $20,000. Equipment, stock and rent deposits would account for $40,000 of the investment, with the remaining money allowed for working capital. The franchise agreement would be of 10 years' duration with a 5 percent royalty paid monthly.

The franchisor/franchisee agreement stipulated that the Flag Shop in Vancouver would supply the franchise stores with ready-made stock. Each franchise store would have to make sure there was a "sewer" in-house who could design and sew flags and pennants. The Atlas manufacturing operation in Vancouver would supply the design and manufacturing knowledge needed for more complicated, special-order products.

In return, the Flag Shop offered the franchisee help with site location, design specifications, equipment and fixtures lists, an operations manual and the training of personnel. After the franchisee's store opened, the corporate support would continue, with national advertising, particularly through the company's *Flag & Banner* quarterly newsletter; new products; management counselling; bookkeeping assistance and group benefits.

That first year, 1987, Braverman sold the Calgary store to a franchisee and one to a franchisee in Victoria. In 1988 two franchises were sold in Ontario.

Currently, Braverman is suggesting that a potential franchisee have a market area of at least 500,000 people. Each store is a free-standing storefront location of around 1,000 square feet. "We realize that our customers are often business people and they want to pull up to a loading area and then quickly drive away. They don't want to have to enter a mall location. Also, malls dictate hours of operation."

Annual sales for the four locations total approximately $2 million. However, Braverman is considering offering mini-shop or seasonal franchises in resort towns. In these cases, the Flag Shop could form part of an already existing, but complementary, retail store. The franchise fee would be lower in these cases.

Meanwhile Braverman intends to open another five franchises by 1990.

16

Piggy-back Franchises

Patrons of the Harvey's hamburger restaurant in Welland, Ontario, might be forgiven for feeling confused as they stare up at the menu board, trying to make a selection. There, among the burgers topped with cheese and bacon, is a whole chicken menu. In fact, what is listed are Swiss Chalet chicken dinners.

At this point the diner might glance around, notice that the staff is in the familiar striped Harvey's uniforms and that there, in the glass counter, is the orderly line of mustard, relish and hot peppers among the condiments to choose from, but still be puzzled by the chicken.

Had the diner read the restaurant sign more closely, he or she would have noticed that Harvey's logo had a smaller Swiss Chalet logo underneath, with the word "serving" connecting the two.

What the customer is seeing is a new trend in franchising called "combination," or "piggybacking," in which two franchise systems are housed under one roof. This particular franchise is known as the "Harvey's Plus." Both Harvey's and Swiss Chalet are owned by the same franchisor, Cara Operations Ltd.

Combination franchising is not to be confused with the

now-familiar side-by-side franchises seen along highways or in strip plazas. When you see, for example, a Tim Horton donuts outlet next to a Wendy's restaurant in a single roadside location, what has often happened is that a single franchisee has simply bought two separate franchises, the objective being to serve the customer a burger and dessert, too.

But, when customers enter a combo or piggyback franchise, they become patrons of two systems, although they are served by staff wearing uniforms of one franchise, and are surrounded by the furnishings of that one franchise system. One franchise is the "host" franchise; the other, the "tenant" franchise.

According to Alexander Konigsberg, a partner with the Montreal-based law firm of Lapointe Goodman, combination franchising is a logical step for franchisors who are looking for a way to expand into smaller markets, or who want to test a product or system without going headlong into a chain-wide system. For example, a Quebec franchisor might want to test a new food product in the Ontario market or a franchisor such as Harvey's might not want to overload a market area with fast-food options. An easy technique would be to place the product in an already existing franchise outlet. The franchisee of the host system gains by having the potential to increase sales.

This potential revenue translates into higher upfront costs for the Harvey's Plus franchise than for the regular Harvey's restaurant. The total investment for a Harvey's will run the franchisee from $570,000 to $1,020,000, with an additional $50,000 upfront franchisee fee, depending on location. In contrast, the total cost for a Harvey's Plus ranges from $767,000 to $1,282,000, with a $75,000 upfront franchise fee.

A large part of the increased cost of the Harvey's Plus is to provide for the kitchen facilities, says Martin Pesken, the vice-president of Harvey's Combo Division. For the franchisee to serve the Swiss Chalet products, he or she needs cooking ovens, cutting tables and larger refrigeration facilities.

In addition, there are increased training costs for the

franchisor. A Harvey's franchisee and his or her key personnel receive up to twelve weeks of training, while the Harvey's Plus people study for up to twenty weeks.

Cara Operations decided to test the combo market back in 1983 as a way to offer both their burger and their chicken items to residents of smaller urban centres, according to Pesken. A total of 14 combos have been opened, mostly in Ontario, but with one each in Alberta and Quebec.

The combos are located not only in centres in which Cara feels that the population is large enough to sustain a burger restaurant, but in those in which a Swiss Chalet with its normal complement of seats might not do well.

If, later, the community were to grow and the company decided to open a Swiss Chalet, the original franchisee would have his geographical area protected, says Pesken. In other words, the community would have to sustain considerable growth.

Pesken says that combination franchising has worked out well for Cara, partly because the company owns both trade marks and systems. But on the question of whether the concept can work well with two completely independent franchise systems, he says, the jury is still out. There are so many problematic areas, areas that could lead to contention, that he thinks the growth of this type of franchising will be slow and cautious.

Konigsberg agrees that combo franchising is still in its infancy. He has attempted several times to negotiate combo deals, only to have the players back away from what amounted to a very confused situation.

The physical space is an immediate area of concern in these negotiations, according to Konigsberg. It is very difficult to obtain agreement over who should own the land or, if the premises are leased, who *controls* it. Neither side wants to be in the situation where the company-manager in a corporate-owned outlet, or a franchisee, might be out in the cold if the host franchisor decided to vacate the premises or if, in an extreme case, the two franchisors had an irreparable falling-out and could not continue to work together.

Then, there are advertising costs to consider. A customer who enters an outlet is not an indicator of advertising effectiveness for either franchisor. Should the two systems pool advertising dollars for these outlets? Surely, one system might have a more extensive, or let's say, national, programme. In the two systems, the franchisees might not even be paying the same percentage of advertising to their franchisors. Will one feel that the other is getting a free ride?

In the area of training, the situation is also hard to resolve. Which franchisor is responsible for the training of the tenant franchisee and who pays this cost? Does this training include confidential information that the tenant franchisor, for example, would rather not disclose?

Protected areas can also lead to heated discussion, according to Konigsberg. The drawing area for one system may need to be much larger than for another. Does this restrict the growth of one system?

Konigsberg suggests that the best advice may be to have a six-month test period after which the arrangement can be terminated. However, such a solution can confuse the consumer who may come to expect to find certain products in the host franchisor's place of business.

In the case of the franchisors with whom Konigsberg worked, the decision taken was to test the concept on company-owned outlets so that there would only be two viewpoints.

What might have resulted, had the deal gone through, would have been granting the host franchisor, assuming the tenant's products were compatible with his or her products, a master franchise. The host franchisor would then have sub-franchised the outlets to its existing franchisees to build into their outlets.

What could be holding up the growth of combination franchising is the desire, on the part of franchisors, to control their own destiny, says Cara's Pesken. "In our case, we control both sides. . . . Whether we would have made these arrangements with another independent franchisor, I don't know."

17

Personnel

Picking the right franchisees for your system is probably the hardest and most unscientific part of a franchisor's job.

Yet, says Cheryl Kostopoulos, vice-president and director of franchising of First Choice Haircutters, the franchisees who make up a franchise system can determine its survival or its downfall.

"Prospective franchisees ask us over and over again why we won't guarantee what their earnings will be," says Kostopoulos. "What we tell them is that we've proven over two hundred times that First Choice Haircutters works as a franchise. Then we add: 'but, we don't know if you will work, in other words, if you will put in the energy, time and commitment that you have promised.' "

Kostopoulos says that whether franchisors are already in business or are at the start of their selection process, a real adjustment is required to realize that franchisees are not employees.

"You can't fire a franchisee," says Kostopoulos. "You cannot order them to change operational policies or decor overnight. You cannot order them to participate in an advertising programme, unless you want to be constantly throwing the franchise agreement back and forth at each other.

"Taking the time to explain a new situation and demonstrate the value of doing things the right way will obtain much better results."

Given the popularity of franchising, the franchisor with an attractive franchise concept to offer has a large pool of talented and resourceful people from whom to choose, according to Toula Sotirakos of Orenstein & Partners in Toronto.

"When the franchisor/franchisee relationship goes sour, it's often because the franchisee wasn't suited to either franchising or to that particular franchise in the first place," says Sotirakos.

"As a franchisor grows in number of outlets, prestige and bottom-line statistics, there is a large escalation in the number of applicants vying for the new locations," she continues.

"Similarly, as the franchisor comes closer to the sold-out point, the competition becomes even fiercer as people want to get a part of the action while they still can.

"However when a franchisor is new and it's not as easy to sell the concept, there has been a tendency in the past for franchisors to be a little less cautious in the selection process."

"I can't stress enough the importance of good franchise recruiting practices," says Karen Castelane, of Woods Gordon. "Good franchisee selection can translate into stability within the system. In turn, that again translates into making it easier for you to recruit other franchisees who suit your system."

According to Castelane, several of the benefits from good franchisee selection include:

1. *Low franchisee turnover.* Reputable, established franchisors report that they try to keep their annual turnover at under 15 percent. They realize that franchisees will sell to make a profit on original investment or retire or seek new challenges. However, the franchisor wants to make money by royalties, which requires that franchisees do well over a period of time, not continuously resell and pay front-end fees.

2. *High unit performance.* A satisfied franchisee will work hard to make the business successful. If the franchisee has a real interest in the product or service of the business, and if he or she has the kind of talent and background necessary for that particular market sector, his or her unit should show positive growth.

3. *Cost savings* (in recruiting and training new personnel). Mature franchisors have training programmes that stretch over several weeks, at least. O'Toole's Roadhouse & Restaurants franchisees, for example, attend a week-long session, and then head-office personnel come to the restaurant for several weeks after it opens.

O'Toole's, with its neighbourhood-style-restaurant approach, illustrates an important point. Many franchisees become well known in their community. Often, in small retail outlets, as opposed to restaurants, the franchise is run by a husband-and-wife team. In small retail outlets, for example, the owner/manager runs the outlet with only one or two other staff members. Unlike corporate-owned stores in which staff are transferred from outlet to outlet, the franchise system has the attraction, for the public, of allowing a personal relationship to develop between owner and customer. Often franchises, whether large or small operations, become well known in the community through sponsorships of baseball teams and charitable events.

"One of the first steps in developing an effective recruiting strategy is to look at your organization – culture, values and philosophy, market targeted for expansion, your business and your franchisees' responsibilities," says Castelane. "From this beginning you can formulate a franchisee profile."

Eligibility characteristics include adequate financial resources (if a prospective franchisee doesn't have the resources, beware!) and a suitable level of education to equip him or her to manage the franchise. The franchisee must have the time necessary to devote to the unit; if, for example, a full-time commitment is required and the franchisee has a nine-to-five day job that he or she can't afford to quit while waiting for the franchise to grow, a manager may be brought in for his unit, but this is not usually as effective as hands-on owner management.

The objective criteria are relatively easy to identify. It's the personality characteristics that are so much harder to qualify and judge, says Castelane.

Doreen Braverman, franchisor of the Flag Shop, has sold five franchises since her decision to franchise in 1987. While her corporate outlet in Vancouver is doing well, as are her franchises in Calgary, Victoria and Ottawa, another franchisee in an Ontario city worked the business for only a few months and then closed the doors. The franchisee cited too much competition and not enough individual freedom as his reasons for leaving the system, says Braverman.

"The most important lesson I have learned in the two years we have been franchising is that the franchisor should check and recheck the personality of the potential franchisee," says Braverman. "It may sound very limiting, but right now I am tending toward selecting people with a military background or at least a background where the person is used to adhering to a predetermined set of rules.

"The franchisor/franchisee relationship certainly has to have room for open discussion and some limited interpretation, but being a franchisee means you accept certain business methods. If you as a franchisee don't want to accept these rules, don't join the system. I also want to make clear to potential franchisees that this is a slow-growth business and that they should be prepared not to really make any money for the first year. Of course, this means I want to make sure I don't accept franchisees who already carry a large debt load. This is a specialized business and it takes time to grow a clientele."

Then there are attitudinal characteristics (good with numbers, understands mechanical aspects of the business, for example) that are just as important as the eligibility requirements. But, according to Castelane, they often receive short shrift when a franchisor considers an applicant.

"When thinking of personality traits, ask yourself: What

do I need to see in my frontline people? After all, these are the people responsible for delivering your product and services. Even more important in consideration: These are the people who create my business public image."

Yet picking the "right" franchisee does not mean that the person has to have a background in your particular industry, though it is helpful. What is most important is that the person is *interested* in the concept.

"Just because a person is all gung ho and eager to join your system doesn't mean that they really understand anything about your industry," says Toula Sotirakos. "The franchisee may not need extensive training in your field. The franchisee may never actually serve a hamburger, cut hair or change a tire. . . . But they still have to understand what makes your business tick. They have to understand what customers expect from this type of business. This should lead to an understanding of *why* this franchise system is successful.

"Yet a potential franchisee's reasons for wanting to be part of your team may have nothing to do with your business. The person's interest may be sparked by totally different influences.

"It may be that their friend is one of your franchisees (and is doing well or at least tells them that she is doing well) or something as simple as that the prospective franchisee has walked by one of your stores dozens of times and has seen the packed parking lots. They are therefore impressed by what they see as your money-making enterprise. But this doesn't mean that your type of business really interests them in their hearts."

Most franchisors are looking for a person who knows and understands business or is willing to learn, agrees Cheryl Kostopoulos. "Our franchisees do not have to be hairdressers to succeed," she says. "They can hire hairdressers. There are other qualities and skills that we are looking for in a potential franchisee."

Hairdressing is a "people" business in terms of both

customers and staff, according to Kostopoulos. Franchisees have to be able to hire, train and motivate their staff while making sure that the customers feel that they are special.

"We definitely discourage the true entrepreneur," says Kostopoulos. "These people will chafe under all the restrictions in the franchise system. Now, that doesn't mean that we don't want someone with initiative and some entrepreneurial bent. We just don't want our head-office staff to spend half their time explaining and arguing about wall coverings and the colour of a sink in our salons.

"We hire interior decorators and other professionals to help us ascertain the colour, size, shape, layout and so on of our stores. We spend thousands of dollars and hours deciding these particulars. We tell our franchisees truthfully that we feel there is a good reason for these decisions. Then we say: Now ... let's get on with making your store successful."

But Stephen MacKneson, franchisor of Sproll's Old Country Bread, says that new franchise systems may differ from more established franchise systems in that they may actually need to recruit entrepreneurial types.

"The attraction of a new franchise system for many people is precisely the risk inherent in the fact that the system is new," says MacKneson. "I'm not saying that a franchisor should go out and look for an entrepreneur who will not tow the line, any more than the franchisee should look for a franchisor who is ill-prepared to offer the proper support.

"But a new system *is* entrepreneurial by virtue of its newness. How else do entrepreneurs make money, except by taking risks?"

In the case of the new franchise system, the franchisor and franchisee are really throwing their hats in the ring together and sharing the hope that the franchise system will exceed their dreams, McKneson says.

Testing a Potential Franchisee
Before a prospective franchisee of First Choice Haircutters

reaches the selection-board stage, he or she takes the Franchi-Zee Evaluation Test (ZET), which provides a professional psychological profile of the prospective franchisee. The test was developed by Margaret Hill, who holds a Master's degree in psychology, specializing in statistics and testing, with assistance from Ross McCallum of Price Waterhouse.

"A lot of people rush into becoming a franchisee because the business *is* a franchise and they have heard so many good reports about franchising," says Hill. "They may also want to buy themselves a job. Alternatively, their goal may be to show the world how important they are. It's very necessary to know what motivates a potential franchisee.

"The prospective franchisee might be the nicest guy in the whole world, but he's not going to be an asset to your system if he's not particularly interested in *your* business," says Hill.

"If a franchisor has an idea of why the franchisee is interested in their particular franchise format it can help the franchisor to formulate a decision about the applicant's suitability," says McCallum. "The more knowledge a franchisor has about a particular applicant, the better the chance to make a good selection."

According to Hill the franchisor who uses the ZET usually has a mature system and has had a few problems with individual franchisees. "It's very seldom that a new franchisor goes to these lengths in qualifying someone," says Hill.

The test consists of 95 written questions, answered over a 20-minute time span. An expanded discussion of some of the traits the test attempts to highlight includes:

- *Entrepreneurship.* The franchisee should be enough of an entrepreneur to seize an opportunity when it arises. In other words, the franchisee must follow rules, but also possess enough initiative to make suggestions and look for new opportunities within the franchise system.
- *Salesmanship.* The importance of selling yourself to the franchisor and later to your staff and customers should not be underestimated.

- *Ambition.* As with any business owner, the franchisee needs to have the ambition to make the business a success.
- *Determination/Perseverance.* Contrary to the expectations of some potential franchisees, it may take many months or even several years before a franchise is profitable. The franchisee has to have the determination to forge through the not-so-good times with a steady eye on the potential for better times ahead.
- *Self-sufficiency.* As Goliger's franchisee Barry Culbert points out, there is a head-office staff available to help franchisees, but this country is vast and the franchisee has to be able to make decisions on his or her own when required.
- *Loyalty and Team Spirit.* In a franchise advertisement in a national newspaper the last line of the copy reads, "No experience needed. Team Players only." Obviously the franchisor of this tree-cutting and pruning service believes that skills can be taught, while the ability to work with others in a common cause has to be part of a person's personality and view of the world.
- *Obedience.* This goes to the very heart of the issue of franchisee selection. A good franchisee follows the rules. Blind obedience is not essential, but the questioning of every head-office decision is unacceptable.

Once a potential franchisee has passed the oral and written tests and seems eminently suitable to be a part of the system, the franchisor has to run with gut feeling.

"This is your franchise system and you know the kind of people you want to represent you," says Sotirakos. "Go with your instincts. Even if a potential franchisee rates number one in every single aspect of your process, but you have a deep-down reluctance to have him on board, it might be a good idea to select another franchisee. Don't forget, this is not an employee. He's not gone out of your system because you want him gone. He's part of your team until his franchisee agreement runs out in 10 or 15 years."

Franchise-Marketing Techniques

According to Karen Castelane, approximately 10 percent of the inquiries a franchisor receives from potential franchisees are serious. Of this number, generally 2 or 3 percent will result in sales. The techniques and avenues available for recruiting franchisees include:

- *Current franchisees.* Probably the best method of recruitment because they know what is required of the system. Your current franchisees are also a living testimonial to the effectiveness of the system.
- *Direct Mail.* Brochures, for example, with tear-out and mail-back portions, allow potential franchisees to express interest with no obligation on their part.
- *Advertisements.* Both locally targeted and national newspaper and radio advertising reaches vast audiences. The problem, of course, is that national advertising is very expensive.
- *Trade shows.* Participation in trade shows is a good way to attract franchisees. Those who attend are at least showing a predisposition to buy a franchise: they got out of their armchairs to be there.
- *Toll-free telephone line.* An 800 number for inquiries makes the franchise system look large, even if it isn't. It generates leads that may not otherwise develop because potential franchisees may not want to incur large long-distance costs as they investigate a number of different franchise systems.

Some franchisors have a very clear portrait of the traits that a franchisee will need to possess to succeed in their system. In the case of Stedmans, a 265-outlet franchised department store chain that stretches from Bonavista on the easternmost point of Newfoundland, to British Columbia, the common threads binding each outlet are that it is situated in a small town and operated by a person who really enjoys being part of a close-knit community. Though there might be a

Stedmans in the small towns surrounding Canada's larger cities, in towns such as Alliston (population 4,845) or Tottenham (population 2,960), we are never going to see a Stedmans outlet chasing the competition on the Yonge Street strip in downtown Toronto, says Gerri Robertson, franchise co-ordinator. It's also highly unlikely we will ever see a Stedmans in a suburban shopping mall, she adds.

The company, which has had dealers since 1912, has targeted 1,100 markets in small towns nation-wide that fit the company's profile. The rank of a town on the suitability scale is determined by current competition (Is there an independent who will not be converted to a Stedmans franchise, and has been there for generations and has the market sewn up?); suitability of location (It must be located on a main street.); and economics (Is the town one-industry and, if so, is that industry healthy?)

Currently the company has more than 130 stores in Ontario, 60 in Atlantic Canada, 50 in western Canada and 25 in Quebec.

The company advertises itself as being "The Business of Small Towns" and is sticking to a particular franchise plan and kind of franchisee that the company knows work well together.

"We advertise our franchise as the one for people who like small-town living," says Robertson. "We are looking for franchisees who want to be part of a community."

While there is no upfront franchise fee, Stedmans franchisees are expected to have equity of approximately $50,000. The total investment for the franchise is in the $160,000 range. Stedmans makes its money by being the main wholesaler to the franchisees.

The franchise-unit profile shows geographical location as towns of from 2,000 to 10,000 people, with a protected area of from 40 to 60 miles. The typical store is about 4,000 square feet and generates about $450,000 in annual sales. Stedmans' total franchise system takes in approximately $75 million a year.

Given that Stedmans advises that a franchisee allot 4 to 6 percent of gross sales for an owner's salary, franchisees in the smaller outlets aren't getting rich. But, then again, the cost of living in small-town Canada is nowhere near that of Vancouver, Calgary, Toronto or Montreal.

Stedmans structures its franchise programme very carefully to attract exactly the kind of small-town–appreciating, hard-working, "want to be your own boss, but can take direction" sort of person who, Robertson says, can feel happy as a Stedmans franchisee.

"It's not uncommon that our franchisees come to us through our established franchisees," says Robertson. "In many cases a person may have to move to a different small town to get a store to operate, but again, that sort of person can integrate into the community fairly quickly."

The Stedmans Game Plan

- *Incentive programmes.* Tips from existing franchisees lead to at least 35 percent of the company's new franchisees. Any current franchisee who suggests a specific person as a dealer receives $2,500 if that person is approved and joins the system. In addition, franchisees receive $2,500 for a tip on any building in an approved market that becomes the home of a new Stedmans. The bottom-line goal of the incentive programme is to convert independent retailers to the Stedman system.

  Since small-town shoppers tend to chat with owners over counters in the store or to stop to chat with other customers, the time a customer spends in the store is significantly longer than in the mall stores of larger urban centres. Each store therefore has an ample stock of well-displayed pamphlets that show the kind of lifestyle a franchisee can expect. (There is a picture of a mother, father and little girl with a church steeple in the background.)

- *Posters.* The company works with local real estate agents to post signs in the windows of vacant stores in small towns, advising that this could be a Stedmans location.

• *Advertisements.* Over 70 percent of the company's recruiting ads are in local newspapers since the company's franchisees generally come from the immediate drawing area.

Being the only game in town does not guarantee success if a store is not well-run. There are specialists in head office for merchandising, marketing, store planning and retail training. The company will go as far as helping a franchisee read a profit-and-loss statement. As Stedmans knows, the franchisee may have the only store of the kind in that town, but the company can never forget that there is another town and another store just down the highway.

The Legalities

18

Disputes

EDWARD N. LEVITT

When franchising works, it can be, for both the franchisor and the franchisee, a "perfect marriage." But, today's franchise marriage, like any business relationship, is generally preceded by carefully drafted legal paperwork. This paperwork is also like a tight pre-nuptial agreement in that, once it is drafted, both signing parties hope that its dispute provisions will never have to be invoked. However, even after all possible eventualities have been dealt with on paper, once the relationship is functioning, disputes can arise. When they do, both the franchisor and franchisee do have legal recourse.

I have both franchisors and franchisees as clients and have examined the documentation from both sides. I also handle disputes. While the legal issues particular to franchising are complex, a number of trends are emerging.

There is no other business method in which there is such a consistently large gap between perception and reality. The inexperienced franchisor looks at established franchise systems and concludes that franchising is a wonderful way to grow wealthy quickly while the franchisees put up all the money and do all the work.

Potential franchisees, in stark contrast, expect to buy into instant success. They are influenced by the commonly held belief that franchisees fare much better than those who start businesses on their own. There are statistics bandied about indicating, for example, that a new independent business has only a 20 percent chance of success, while a new franchise has an 80 percent chance, but the reality is somewhat different. There are no Canadian statistical studies dealing with the success rate of new franchises, but the 80-percent figure is probably true for established franchise systems only. The numbers may not hold true for young franchise systems, many of which open a few outlets, never get off the ground and quietly expire.

An example of this situation occurred with the Loh's Ice Cream franchise system, which grew, with much fanfare and even a public offering on the Vancouver Stock Exchange, to a grand total of eight stores. At that point it ran out of money and quietly closed its operations, leaving the franchisees to sink or swim on their own.

Since there is no legislation specifically designed for franchising (except in Alberta), the outcome of legal disputes is determined by general business law. Franchising, however, has its peculiarities, which as it becomes more popular and disputes more frequent, the legal community is gradually coming to recognize.

The base and strength of the franchise concept is that the franchisor has a good name, identifiable image and effective business method that he or she is prepared to let selected persons use for a specified time, upon certain terms and conditions and in accordance with strict rules and regulations. What complicates matters and makes franchising unique is the fact that the franchisee is an independent business person. So, a situation develops in which there are two independent business people legally and practically tied to each other, able to dramatically affect each other's lives, but at the same time pursuing their own goals and objectives.

Other aspects of franchising that set it apart from other business or commercial relationships, and are taken into account in the resolution of legal disputes, are the usually unequal business experience and financial resources of the parties involved. Some franchisees may have the business background, money and intestinal fortitude to do battle with a franchisor, but most don't. In many franchise disputes to date, the franchisee's lack of either money or willpower to sustain a long legal battle has been an important factor.

There are few commercial situations in which the stakes are so high. Often the franchisee is middle-aged, has recently quit a job that he or she has held for a long time and has invested the savings of a lifetime in the franchise opportunity. The franchisee's hope and objective is to be able to utilize his or her remaining productive years to earn a sufficient return on investment to retire comfortably. For such a franchisee, a serious dispute with the franchisor is almost "life threatening."

Equally for the franchisor, particularly if new, a dispute with a franchisee threatens life-sustaining cash flow in the form of royalties, goodwill, reputation among the trade and the value of franchise trade marks. In addition, the outcome of a dispute with one franchisee can drastically affect the franchisor's relationship with other franchisees in the system. When one realizes that the principal assets, if not the only assets, of most franchisors are their trade marks and franchise agreements, it is not surprising that a franchisor often regards every serious dispute as a contest that cannot be lost. When franchise disputes reach the courts, the judge has to balance these contradictory needs and the very legitimate rights both parties are seeking to protect.

In the United States, franchise-specific legislation and a pronounced tendency to head to the courtroom to resolve differences are notable facts of life. In Canada, it has been rare for a franchise dispute to be resolved by litigation. Recently, however, the number of Canadian court cases dealing with franchise issues has significantly increased. The dramatic rise in franchising activity over the last five to 10 years may be largely responsible.

Often disputes arise because the franchisor misunderstands what franchising can realistically achieve. He or she underestimates the time, effort and money required to develop a solid franchise network. The franchisee, in turn, is in such a rush to jump on the bandwagon, that he or she may not have investigated thoroughly the franchisor's capability.

Successful franchise systems do not develop overnight. Usually, they evolve over several, if not many, years. The growth rate in the early years is usually slow and increases gradually. Potential franchisors often focus on the rapid growth of systems that have become established and misunderstand how long it took. They hear stories of franchisors opening 30 or more units in a single year, but fail to realize that while such rapid expansion is an indication of success in a mature franchise system, it is a sign of trouble to come, as unmanageable growth, for a new one.

An often-fatal mistake made by first-time franchisors is to underestimate the amount of money needed to launch a successful franchise expansion. They may look to the front-end franchise fees to bolster their capital requirements and miss the fact that, at best, these fees will cover the real costs to a franchisor of finding the franchisee, negotiating the franchise agreement, finding the location, negotiating the lease, training the franchisee, helping with the establishment of the unit and supporting the franchisee through the first few months of transition. Perhaps the most common misperception concerns the time it takes for a franchisor to see real profits from the system. It comes as a shock to find out that a franchisor may need as many as 10 units operating in the black just to break even.

A psychological phenomenon that may be unique to franchising is another source of problems and disputes. In almost every system the franchisees start out feeling very dependent upon the franchisor. They generally look to the franchisor as the source of all knowledge concerning the business. This situation changes at some point, in most systems. Some franchisees, often the more successful ones, come to believe that their success is mostly attributable to their own efforts and start to view the franchisor's activities as intrusive and unnecessary. In extreme cases, the franchisees may come to believe that they have a better way of running their businesses, even the franchise system as a whole, and that the franchisor is making a number of significant errors. Regardless of who is right and who is wrong, some of the most hotly contested battles emerge from this situation.

The very success and increased acceptability of franchising is contributing to an increase in disputes, as better-educated, more-experienced and economically stronger individuals buy franchises. These franchisees have higher expectations and are much more likely to be combative if problems arise.

There may come a time in the growth of a franchise system, when, because of developments in the market-place or other reasons known to the franchisor, the franchisor attempts to make changes throughout the system in such fundamental areas as the products or services offered by the franchisees, advertising programmes, promotional campaigns, store appearances, trade marks and pricing. At such times, the franchisor may become acutely aware of the differences between employees and franchisees. Employees can simply be told what changes to make; franchisees must be persuaded. To effect significant (and sometimes even minor) changes in a franchise network, the franchisor has to possess the skills of a politician, statesman and labour negotiator. When these skills are lacking, disputes frequently occur.

When franchisees complain about franchisors, the issues raised most often are the franchisors' choice of a poor location, the lack of operational support, the lack of or ineffectiveness of national or regional advertising programmes, the unnecessarily high cost of inventories and supplies where the franchisor (as is often the case) controls or determines the source of supply, and the lack of leadership on the part of the franchisor when significant developments occur in the market-place.

Sometimes the franchisee's complaints arise from the

encroachment by the franchisor or other franchisees upon the franchisee's territory.

The complaints of the franchisor are often about the franchisee's failing to maintain the system image, selling unauthorized products or services, operating in a sub-standard manner or withholding payment for royalties, advertising contributions, rent, inventory or supplies.

But in spite of all precautions, disputes do occur. Often these disputes are resolved by negotiation and compromise. Sometimes the franchisor decides that it is better to let a rebellious franchisee alone than to risk the financial cost and adverse publicity that result from litigation. The franchisor can ride out the term of the franchise agreement and then refuse to renew. In rare cases, a franchisee may be allowed to break away from the system and continue as an independent at the same location. This step might be taken to rid the system of a "bad apple" that could otherwise ruin the "whole barrel."

But by far the most popular resolution has been for the franchisor and the franchisee to agree to end the relationship. Then, usually, the unit is sold to a new, and perhaps more co-operative, franchisee. Alternatively, the franchisor may decide to buy the unit back from the franchisee in order to operate it as a corporate unit, or to be refranchised down the road.

In many disputes, who retains the business location is often a major issue. This is especially true in retail operations, restaurants and fast-food outlets. As a result, it is common for franchisors to structure their franchise agreements so that they control the location if serious problems arise. Often this is accomplished by the franchisor taking the head lease and subletting to the franchisee, with cross-termination provisions being inserted in the sub-lease and franchise agreement. In this way, the franchisor is given the right to cancel the sub-lease and regain possession of the business premises if the franchise agreement is terminated.

Less frequently, the franchisor allows the franchisee to take the lease directly from the landlord, but requires the franchisee to agree in writing that the franchisor has the discretionary right to have the lease assigned to him or her if the franchise agreement is cancelled for any reason.

Most often, once it has been decided which party will remain in possession of the business premises, a negotiated settlement follows soon after, for the party in possession of the business in a franchise dispute has a decided strategic advantage. For example, the dispossessed franchisee may lose his or her principal source of income with the premises, while the franchisor must put up with continuing damage to the reputation of the system and to his or her relationship with the other franchisees in the system, if the franchisee cannot be ousted from the franchised unit.

Unfortunately, we are currently witnessing an increase in franchise disputes, and the trend will accelerate in the near future. The increase in the number of court cases can be attributed to, if nothing else, the increased volume of franchising in recent years. But that is not the entire story. Today there is a virtual flood of new franchisors. A disturbing number of them, although presumably well-intentioned, have little or no experience in the business being franchised. They too often embark upon a franchise programme without sufficient capital, knowledge or commitment. Their business may not even be franchisable.

In more and more instances, a business born today is offered for sale as a franchise tomorrow. There are two distinct bodies of knowledge necessary for a successful franchise system; knowledge about the business itself and knowledge about the business of franchising. Weaknesses in either area will lead to problems and disputes in the franchise relationship.

The franchisee, unlike the independent business person, can be drawn into obligations that were not anticipated, simply by virtue of being a franchisee. This is particularly true in labour-law developments involving franchise systems.

Franchisees of Canada Post found themselves in this situation. The franchisees had to bear the increased labour costs as the courts decided that each franchisee was a successor to Canada Post's business and therefore bound by the existing collective-bargaining agreement to which Canada Post was a party. This development has all but eroded Canada Post's plans to franchise its post-office network.

From a judicial point of view, there is no special conclusion or result to be drawn from the simple fact that one is, say, a franchisee or a franchisor, or that the relationship arises from a franchise agreement. Rather, general principles of law, most particularly contract law, are applied to franchise situations or facts.

However, in many cases, franchisees have been able to win the sympathy of the judge, because of the poor conduct of the franchisor.

Some people believe that a franchisee, like a consumer in a dispute with a corporation, will always have an edge with the court on the basis that "David" is in need of protection against "Goliath." Judges, however, are not automatically so disposed. Again and again, franchisors have been able to succeed against their franchisees in court.

This trend was demonstrated by the Pizza Delight case in British Columbia. In that case, the franchisee succumbed to the "I really did it myself" syndrome some franchisees experience and attempted to break away from the franchised pizza chain without justification. The court did not hesitate to award the franchisor significant damages for the franchisee's breach of the franchise agreement.

What will the future hold for franchise disputes and litigation? Although franchise legislation may eventually be put in place in provinces other than Alberta, the intertwined nature of the franchisor/franchisee relationship will continue to give rise to disputes. There are just too many variables and too many differences among franchisors, among franchisees and among the businesses being franchised.

There are a number of traits franchisors and franchisees

should watch out for when considering a franchise relationship. Failure to heed these signs can lead to grief.

Traits of a Bad Franchisor

• *Is undercapitalized.* The franchisor expects to pay overheads, expand the system and earn a profit from the front-end franchise fees.

• *Sells franchises to the first warm body.* The franchisor does not investigate the applicant thoroughly, and does not require adherence to a sound franchisee profile.

• *Opens units anywhere and everywhere without regard for any specified site criteria.*

• *Expands over too wide a geographical area.* For example, the franchisor sets up three stores in Vancouver and a fourth in Toronto.

• *Organization has no depth of management.* For example, the franchise originator and spouse may be doing all the training, buying, site selection, advertising, and so on by themselves.

• *Expands too quickly.* The franchisor is therefore incapable of supporting every franchisee in the system.

• *More concerned about cash flow, image and contract points than about the profitability of the franchisee.*

• *Lacks experience in the business, in franchising or in both.*

Traits of a Bad Franchisee

• *Attracted to the franchise primarily as an investment, rather than as the operator and investor.*

• *Underfinanced and consequently incapable of weathering a slow startup or changes in the market-place.*

• *Too independent.* The franchisee is unlikely to follow guidelines and rules.

• *Has unrealistic expectations about the financial benefits of or the demands made by the franchised business.*

• *Too dependent on others and needs too much guidance.*

• *Personality is not suitable for the business.* A shy person, for example, should not buy a franchise that requires strong selling skills.

• *Lacks stability in his or her personal life or receives no moral support from his or her family.*

19

Franchise Documentation

EDWARD N. LEVITT

Franchising is one of the best things to have ever happened to the pulp-and-paper industry. There is nothing like a vibrant franchise system to generate paper. In the preparation, negotiation and administration of the franchise documents, freedom of contract is the supreme doctrine. For the franchisee, there may be some solace in certain rules of construction, such as *contra proferentum*, which resolves any ambiguities in a form agreement, i.e., one that is not usually to be negotiated, against the party who prepared it, and the knowledge that the courts may be somewhat sympathetic toward the weaker franchisee (if it can be shown that the franchisor treated the franchisee unfairly). However, in the main, the franchisee will have to live with the bargain struck as set out in the franchise documents. For the franchisor, it is important to ensure that the documents delineate the business deal thoroughly and unambiguously and provide the remedies needed to protect the franchisor and the system if the relationship breaks down.

Application Form

Most often a franchisor requires prospective franchisees to complete a franchise application form before the applicant is given any documents or financial information. This form is usually the first document the franchisee's lawyer sees. More often than not, it is already signed by the time the lawyer receives it, and therefore the lawyer has no chance to address any problems for the client. The application usually calls for personal and financial information about the applicant. It also generally contains secrecy and confidentiality provisions to protect the franchisor against the possibility that the applicant will use the information subsequently gained about the franchised business for his or her own purposes. In addition, the application form almost always requires a deposit to be lodged by the applicant. Usually, this is a "good faith" deposit, ranging from a few hundred to a few thousand dollars, and is refundable if a deal is not consummated. In such cases, however, some franchisors deduct certain costs associated with the application process, for example, real estate fees for obtaining the site and the costs of investigating the applicant. If the applicant is dealing with a new franchise system, consideration might be given to having the franchisor's lawyer hold the deposit in trust.

Franchise Agreement

The franchise agreement is the corner-stone document in any franchise system. It contains crucial provisions, which are determined by the business goals and policies of the particular franchise system and by the nature of the business being franchised. For example, there will be differences between a franchise agreement used in the franchising of a service business and one used where the franchised business is, say, a fast-food outlet. Some franchise agreements merely license the franchisee to use certain trade marks in a defined area. Other franchise agreements dictate every specific aspect of the business to be conducted at a chosen location. These latter franchises are commonly known as "business format" franchises. The key provisions of a typical business-format franchise agreement are described below, from the point of view of both the franchisor and the franchisee.

1. *The parties*: For tax and liability reasons, the franchisee may wish to have the franchise granted to a corporation. The franchisor rarely objects to this approach, but usually requires the franchisee to personally guarantee the corporation's obligations, financial and otherwise, under *all* of the franchise documents. It is also advisable for the franchisor to exact a covenant requiring the individual to remain the controlling shareholder. If the franchisee is to be a partnership, similar restrictions on the change of control of the partnership would be in order.

2. *Site*: Sometimes a franchisor will sell a franchise without first having selected a site for the unit. In such a case, the franchise agreement or a collateral agreement should ensure that the franchisee and the franchisor have a means of unwinding the transaction, in the event that an acceptable site is not selected within a reasonable period of time. In most situations, the franchisor must be satisfied, in his or her sole discretion, that the site is acceptable.

3. *Exclusive Territory*: While it is not uncommon for a franchise agreement to provide for protected, exclusive territory for the franchisee, this approach is not mandatory. Some franchisors, particularly in the more mature franchise systems such as McDonald's and Colonel Sanders Kentucky Fried Chicken, will not give the franchisee an exclusive area and will insist that the franchise is for a specific location only. However, it is important for a franchisee to have some assurance that another franchise in the system or another store owned by the franchisor will not be established in such close proximity as to draw customers from the market needed to support the franchisee's business. When a franchise system is first being developed, it is difficult to know how wide such exclusive territories should be. Franchisors are often too generous with the size of the territories in the early days. Frequently, exclusive territories are defined as

being within a certain radius of the business premises of the franchisee or by municipal boundaries. It should be kept in mind, however, that traffic patterns and population density can be as important or more important than geographical area.

4. *Term and renewal*: The length of the term of the franchise agreement, I believe, is a function of the amount of money being invested by the franchisee. The franchisee will want a sufficiently long term to recoup his or her investment and earn a reasonable rate of return. Often the term of a franchise is from 10 to 20 years. However, there is a trend to shorter franchise terms, which parallels a similar trend in retail leases. It is advisable for the franchisor to split the desired franchise term into segments of, say, 5 or 10 years, with renewal provisions subject to specific renewal criteria. These criteria can give the franchisor the opportunity to get rid of a franchisee who is not in technical breach of the agreement, but who may not have been abiding by the spirit of the agreement or the franchise relationship. On renewal, the franchisor can also reserve the right to adjust royalty and advertising rates or require a further franchise fee. On the part of the franchisee, it is most important that these criteria be objective and realistic.

5. *Breach and termination*: All franchise agreements must have clear and comprehensive provisions outlining what will be considered a breach of the agreement. The consequences of such a breach should also be thoroughly set out. Termination will be one of those consequences, and the events to follow termination, such as repurchase of assets by the franchisor and non-competition on the part of the franchisee, should be dealt with. The franchisor will often reserve the right to repurchase the franchisee's business assets in order to continue the operation at the particular location. The franchisee's concern will be that the formula chosen for valuing these assets is fair.

The franchisee will also want to have the right to receive notice of the default, specifying how the default can be rectified and providing a reasonable time to cure it.

6. *Front-end fees*: The front-end fees charged by franchisors are used to reimburse the franchisor for the cost of finding the franchisee, selecting a site, negotiating the lease, training the franchisee and providing assistance in opening and establishing the business. Occasionally, there may even be an element of profit in the front-end fee. The amount of this fee has to be decided with care and only after thorough financial analysis. As the system grows and matures and there is an increased demand for franchises, the front-end fee can be increased. Frequently, the front-end fee in new franchises is set at $15,000 to $25,000.

7. *Ongoing royalty fees*: Ongoing royalty fees are the life-blood of any franchise system. They are usually payable periodically, such as monthly or weekly, and are usually determined as a percentage of gross revenue. Such fees should be sufficient to provide the franchisor with the desired return, while at the same time allowing the franchisee to prosper. The rate for such royalties can differ greatly from one franchise system to another, but is usually between 4 and 8 percent of gross revenue.

8. *Advertising contributions*: A central concept in most franchise systems is the national or regional advertising pool. The franchise agreement usually provides that the franchisee will contribute to an advertising fund to be administered by the franchisor. The amount of such contribution will vary, but most often it is between 1 and 3 percent of the gross revenue of the franchisee. In dealing with a newer franchise system, it might benefit the franchisee to have a provision by which the franchisee is not required to contribute to an advertising fund until a minimum number of units has been established in the system, and requiring the stores owned by the franchisor to contribute on a pro-rata basis.

9. *Purchases by the franchisee*: Some franchise systems, by their nature, require that the franchisee purchase all inventory from the franchisor, for example, where the franchisee sells clothing produced under only one label. In many franchise systems, the franchisees are required to purchase equipment from suppliers designated by the franchisor. Similarly, they may be required to purchase inventories and supplies from designated suppliers, or they may be permitted to purchase elsewhere subject to approval by the franchisor. In this area, the franchisor's interest is to control quality and assure buying power for the system; the franchisee's interest is to be assured of consistent and reliable supplies at reasonable prices.

10. *Construction of the franchised unit*: The franchisor must decide whether to allow the franchisee to build the franchised unit (strictly in accordance with prescribed plans and specifications), or to build for the franchisee on a "turnkey" basis, for example, providing a completely finished unit, ready to do business. Some franchisors earn additional revenues by charging the franchisees a significant mark-up on the construction. Other franchisors take on such construction simply to assure consistency throughout the system. Ideally, the franchisor's greater expertise and buying power will enable him or her to construct the unit for the franchisee more cheaply than could the franchisee. From the franchisee's perspective, it is advisable, whether in the franchise agreement or by a collateral document, that the franchisor be required to state the construction price or formula for calculating it, and to accept the usual general-contractor provisions, such as doing the work in a good and workman-like fashion. It is also appropriate for the franchisor to provide customary warranties for work done and materials supplied.

11. *Training*: Both the franchisor and the franchisee have a substantial interest in the training process. The franchisee wants to learn all there is to know about operating the

particular business and the franchisor wants to ensure that the right people are well trained to be operators in the system. The provisions of the franchise agreement dealing with training most often require the franchisee to participate in a specified training programme and to complete that programme to the satisfaction of the franchisor. In addition, the franchisor will want to have the right to require the franchisee and his or her staff to undergo periodic retraining. Usually, the franchisee is required to pay for travel and lodging costs, but there is no fee charged for the initial training. Of concern to a franchisee are training provisions that require the franchisee and/or his or her staff to travel too frequently to the franchisor's distant training centre for retraining.

12. *Trade marks*: It is customary to insert provisions confirming the ownership by the franchisor of the system trade marks and regulating the use of the marks by the franchisee. The franchisee might want to see provisions according to which the franchisor agrees to defend and indemnify the franchisee from any action by others for infringement of their trade marks.

13. *Operating standards*: Virtually all franchise agreements contain extensive provisions requiring the franchisee to operate the franchise strictly according to the standards and procedures set by the franchisor. Often there is a reference to the operating manual as the document that contains the operating standards and procedures that must be followed by the franchisee. All franchise systems change over time, if for no other reason, because of market changes and innovations in the particular industry. Accordingly, the franchisor has some interest in retaining the right to alter the system standards and procedures to accommodate such changes and innovations, and to require the franchisees to abide by the new standards and procedures. A problem can arise, however, when the franchise system is new and the changes are too frequent and substantial. This may occur because the

franchisor is not experienced enough to structure the business and the franchise system in the best way. The franchisee might want to consider an annual limit on the frequency and cost of such changes.

14. *Assignment*: Some franchise agreements provide that the franchise is strictly personal to the franchisee and is not assignable to others. Most often, however, the franchisee is permitted to sell the franchise to others, subject to the franchisor's prior approval. The franchisee will want a provision requiring the franchisor to act reasonably in granting such approval. It is advisable for a franchise agreement to provide for a transfer fee to compensate the franchisor for the expenses he or she will incur on an assignment for training the assignee, executive time, lost revenue as the assignee learns the business, and legal, investigative and accounting costs.

Sub-lease

In many franchise systems, particularly fast-food franchises, good locations are extremely valuable. Accordingly, many franchisors will want to maintain control over the locations by taking a head lease and sub-leasing to the franchisee. In these situations, the franchisor will want to develop a standard form sub-lease and add it as a schedule to the franchise agreement.

Registered-User Agreement

Trade marks are usually an important part of any franchise system. To protect a franchisor's proprietary rights in a trade mark, the trade mark is often registered under the Federal Trademarks Act. In these circumstances, each franchisee will be required to execute a user agreement, which is registered with the Registrar of Trademarks.

Security Agreement

To secure payment of monies owed by the franchisee to the franchisor, the franchisor may require the franchisee to execute some type of security document giving the franchisor a charge on some or all of the business assets of the franchisee. This approach is particularly useful where the franchisor supplies the franchisee with inventory or supplies on an ongoing basis.

Equipment and Sign Leases

Sometimes, the leasing of equipment and signs is an alternative financing approach chosen by franchisors for their franchisees. The leasing may be done through third-party lessors or the franchisor. In either case, the franchisor should have the ability to retake the leases or equipment (through cross-termination provisions with the franchise agreement) upon a termination of the franchise relationship.

Development, Master or Territorial Franchise Agreements

From time to time, situations arise in which the franchisee is to be given rights to establish more than one franchised unit in a particular geographical area. These rights might be exclusive or non-exclusive, take the form of rights of first refusal or options and may be tied to certain performance criteria or a minimum number of unit openings over a given period of time. Frequently these rights are contained in an agreement called a franchise development agreement, master franchise agreement or territorial franchise agreement; the labels are really unimportant. Sometimes, the franchisee is given the right to sub-franchise to others within the designated territory. While these types of agreements are beyond the scope of this book, you should be aware that they exist and that they are often more specialized and vary greatly from situation to situation.

The franchise relationship is complex and challenging. In a franchise system, the franchisees acquire the temporary use of the franchisor's name and methods of doing business. The maintenance of consistent quality of products and services is essential, and each unit in the system must project a similar, if not identical, image. In these circumstances, detailed documentation is inevitable. The aspects of such documentation outlined above should be regarded as general information and not as advice for any particular situation. Anyone contemplating the development of a franchise system or the purchase of a franchise should consult a lawyer experienced in franchising.

Appendix A

The Canadian Franchise Association
In Canada, there is only one association dedicated to the franchise industry. This is the Canadian Franchise Association, a 300-member organization based in Toronto. The CFA also has affiliates in Montreal and Vancouver.

Founded in 1967, the association's mandate is first and foremost to promote ethical and responsible business practices among franchisors. A secondary role is to represent member franchisors to government, the general public and the media.

As a potential franchisor, the CFA can function for you as a support system. As a prospective franchisee, association staff can answer general questions about franchising.

The association also holds seminars regularly for its members and encourages networking. In addition, the CFA also holds seminars open to the public to encourage an understanding of the franchise concept.

But the CFA can also help with questions about American and overseas franchisors through its ongoing dialogue with similar franchise associations in 16 other countries. So if you are wondering about a franchise system that is coming into Canada, or if you are considering buying the rights to bring a particular foreign-based franchise system to our country, the CFA may be able to answer some questions for you.

While not belonging to the association does not mean that a particular franchise is not a credible, responsible franchisor, prospective franchisees might consider checking to see if a franchisor does belong.

In joining the association the franchisor agrees to adhere to a Code of Ethics. The association is self-policing but membership does show at least a willingness to adhere to the code. In fact, there is a place on the Code of Ethics Certificate of Membership for an authorized person from the franchisor's organization to sign to signify acceptance of the code.

A regular member of the association has to have been in business AS A FRANCHISOR for at least 3 years and have at least 3 franchised outlets up and running. An associate member must be in the business of franchising or have demonstrated an intention to engage in franchising.

Moreover, the association has affiliate members who supply products or services to franchisors. So if you as a potential franchisor or franchisee are looking for a lawyer, management consultant, accountant or banker who really knows franchising, this is a good place to start your search for professionals who specialize in the field.

Appendix B

Consultants
With the popularity of franchising, there has emerged a whole battalion of business people eager to serve as franchise consultants. Often it is as difficult to choose a franchise consultant as it is to choose a franchise system. What follows is an adapted version of the proposed guidelines for retaining a franchise consultant as suggested by The Canadian Franchise Association.

Is the consultant a member of the Canadian Franchise Association? Whether or not, does the consultant adhere to the CFA Code of Ethics, and the CFA Ethical Advertising Code?

Who are the principals of the franchise consultant business? What are their professional and business backgrounds and qualifications?

How long has the consultant been engaged in the consulting business? Can he provide references?

What are the financial resources of the consultant?

Does the consultant maintain an office, or does he simply generate business through advertising?

Has the consultant ever been involved in professional,

business or similar presentations with others in the franchise industry? If so, references and details should be obtained.

Is the consultant prepared to give a firm advance estimate as to what fees would be incurred and to state what part of the work is to be performed by the consultant's organization and what part will be sub-contracted?

Does the work involved include services for which the consultant is not professionally qualified, for example, legal and accounting services? If so, who will perform these services, and are such persons professionally qualified? Is the consultant prepared to work with other professional advisors of the client, for example, the client's lawyers, accountants and real estate and business brokers?

If eventual expansion is contemplated in the Province of Quebec, does the consulting firm have bilingual capabilities?

Appendix C

To Sign or Not?
The following checklist, courtesy of the Federal Business
Development Bank, is a final guide to consider before signing
on the dotted line.

THE FRANCHISEE:	YES	NO
Do you know why you want to buy a franchise?	☐	☐
Are you relating your interests to the right type of franchise?	☐	☐
Do you have the physical and educational requirements to be a franchisee?	☐	☐
Is your work experience related in any way to the type of franchise you want to buy?	☐	☐
Do you have good learning abilities?	☐	☐
Are you prepared for hard work and financial risks?	☐	☐
Can you manage staff?	☐	☐
Can you work under rules and controls to be specified by the franchisor?	☐	☐

THE FRANCHISOR:		
Do you know who the principals are?	☐	☐

Do you know their personal and business history and is it related to the franchise? ☐ ☐

THE FRANCHISE OPERATIONS:

Are the franchise operations well established? ☐ ☐

Is it a growing business with an indicated good future? ☐ ☐

Do you know what the franchisor owns or controls (trade name, trademark, product, process)? ☐ ☐

Have you found out the names and addresses of other established franchisees? ☐ ☐

Have you visited and talked with these other franchisees? ☐ ☐

Sales and profit:

Have you estimated sales, expenses, and profit and, if possible, compared them to an existing franchise? ☐ ☐

Has a professional accountant helped you? ☐ ☐

Have you studied the market? ☐ ☐

Have you assessed your share of the market? ☐ ☐

Location and premises:

Can you choose your location? ☐ ☐

Is your location the best one for you? ☐ ☐

Are there standards for location and premises specified by the franchisor? ☐ ☐

Can you make any adaptations to the location and premises? ☐ ☐

Do you know if you must lease or buy your premises? ☐ ☐

If so, have you checked the terms? ☐ ☐

Equipment, fixtures, layout:

Are the equipment and fixtures specified? ☐ ☐

Must you buy or lease the specific equipment and fixtures only from the franchisor? ☐ ☐

If so, are the terms and prices reasonable compared to other sources? ☐ ☐

Is the layout specified by the franchisor? ☐ ☐

Can you make adaptations to the layout? ☐ ☐

Protection of territory:

Is your territory well defined? ☐ ☐

Do you know how your territory is protected? ☐ ☐

Can your territory be reduced or expanded? ☐ ☐

Purchase costs:

Do you know what the franchise fee entitles you to? ☐ ☐

Is the franchise fee a one-time payment? ☐ ☐

Have you checked for royalties and service charges? ☐ ☐

Do you know who pays for the legal fees, permits, licences and insurance? ☐ ☐

Have you made financial arrangements for equipment and premises? ☐ ☐

Can you arrange financing with the franchisor? ☐ ☐

Training:

Will the franchisor train you and your staff? ☐ ☐

If so, do you know who pays for this? ☐ ☐

Prices and sales:

Are prices set by the franchisor? ☐ ☐

Can you adjust the prices or offer special discounts? ☐ ☐

Are there sales quotas and are they realistic? ☐ ☐

Do you know what happens if you don't reach the quotas? ☐ ☐

Product and supplies:

Must you carry all the franchisor's product lines? ☐ ☐

Can you stock product lines other than the franchisor's? ☐ ☐

Is the source for products and supplies specified? ☐ ☐

Can you arrange terms for the products and supplies? ☐ ☐

Business controls:

Has the franchisor specified rules and regulations in running your franchise? ☐ ☐

Do you know what all the rules and regulations are? ☐ ☐

Are you in agreement with them? ☐ ☐

Can these rules and regulations be adjusted? ☐ ☐

THE FRANCHISE CONTRACT:

Do you understand all clauses of the contract? ☐ ☐

Is everything that you want written in the contract? ☐ ☐

Have you especially checked the conditions of termination, bankruptcy, transfer, renewal, and sale? ☐ ☐

Has your lawyer carefully read each clause and explained it to you? ☐ ☐

Appendix D

Other Sources of Information
The following is a list of government offices where information on franchising may be found:

ALBERTA
Department of Economic Development and Trade
Sterling Place Bldg.
9940-106 St.
Edmonton, Alberta
T5K 2P6

BRITISH COLUMBIA
Ministry of Industry and Small Business Development
1045 Douglas St.
Victoria, British Columbia
V8W 3C1

MANITOBA
Department of Business Development and Tourism
155 Carlton St.
Winnipeg, Manitoba
R3C 3H8

NEW BRUNSWICK
Department of Commerce and Technology
Centennial Building

P.O. Box 6000
Fredericton, New Brunswick
E3B 5H1

NEWFOUNDLAND AND LABRADOR
Department of Development and Tourism
4th Floor S., West Block
Confederation Building
St. John's, Newfoundland
A1C 5T7

NORTHWEST TERRITORIES
Department of Economic Development and Tourism
P.O. Box 1320
Yellowknife, Northwest Territories
X1A 2L9

NOVA SCOTIA
Department of Industry, Trade and Technology
World Trade and Convention Centre
1800 Argyle St., 7th Floor
P.O. Box 519
Halifax, Nova Scotia
B3J 2R7

ONTARIO
Ministry of Industry, Trade and Technology
Hearst Block
900 Bay St.
Toronto, Ontario
M7A 2E1

PRINCE EDWARD ISLAND
Department of Industry
Shaw Building, P.O. Box 2000
Charlottetown, P.E.I.
C1A 7N8

QUEBEC
Ministère de l'Industrie du Commerce et de la
Technologie
710 Place D'Youville
Québec, Quebec
G1R 4Y4

SASKATCHEWAN
Department of Economic Development and Tourism
Bank of Montreal Building
2103–11th Ave.
Regina, Saskatchewan
S4P 3V7

When investigating the franchisor, you can obtain information from several sources:

- Canadian Franchise Association
  88 University Ave., Suite 607
  Toronto, Ont.
  M5J 1T8
  (416) 595-5005

- Dun & Bradstreet Report on the Company
  (Obtained from your bank)

- The Better Business Bureau

- Alberta Securities Commission
  10th Floor, Capital Square Building
  Edmonton, Alberta
  (403) 427-5201

- Federal Trade Commission (FTC)
  6th and Pennsylvania Ave. N.W.
  Washington, D.C. 20580
  (202) 376-2805
  (Disclosure statement if franchisor operating in U.S.A.)

Further Reading

Business Building Ideas For Franchises and Small Business
by M. Serif
(Pilot Industries
103 Cooper Street
Babylon, New York 11702)

The Complete Handbook of Franchising
by D.D. Seltz
(Addison-Wesley)
$49.95

The Dow Jones-Irwin Guide To Franchises
by Peter G. Norback and Craig T. Norback
(Dow Jones-Irwin)
$17.50

Franchising
by William L. Siegel
(Wiley PR)
$8.95

Franchising in Canada–Pros and Cons
by Michael Coltman

(International Self-Counsel Press Ltd.–Toronto)
$6.95

Franchising, The Inside Story
by John Kinch
(Tri Mark Publishing Co. Inc.
184 Quigley Boulevard
Wilmington, Delaware 19850)

How To Franchise Your Business
by Mack Lewis
(Pilot Industries Inc.
347 Fifth Avenue
New York, New York 10016)

The Insider's Guide to Franchising
by Bryce Webster
(Amacon
American Management Association
135 West 50th Street
New York, New York 10020)

International Franchising: An Overview
M. Mendelsohn (Editor)
(Elsevier)
$59.25

Selecting The Best Franchises
by Gregory Kravitt
(Down Jones-Irwin)

The Successful Franchise: A Working Strategy
Golden Square Service Ltd.
(Gower Publishing Co.)
$29.50

Understanding Franchise Contracts
by David Hjelmfelt
(Pilot Industries
103 Cooper Street
Babylon, New York 11702)

Woman's Guide to Her Own Franchised Business
by Anne Small
(Pilot Industries
103 Cooper Street
Babylon, New York 11702)

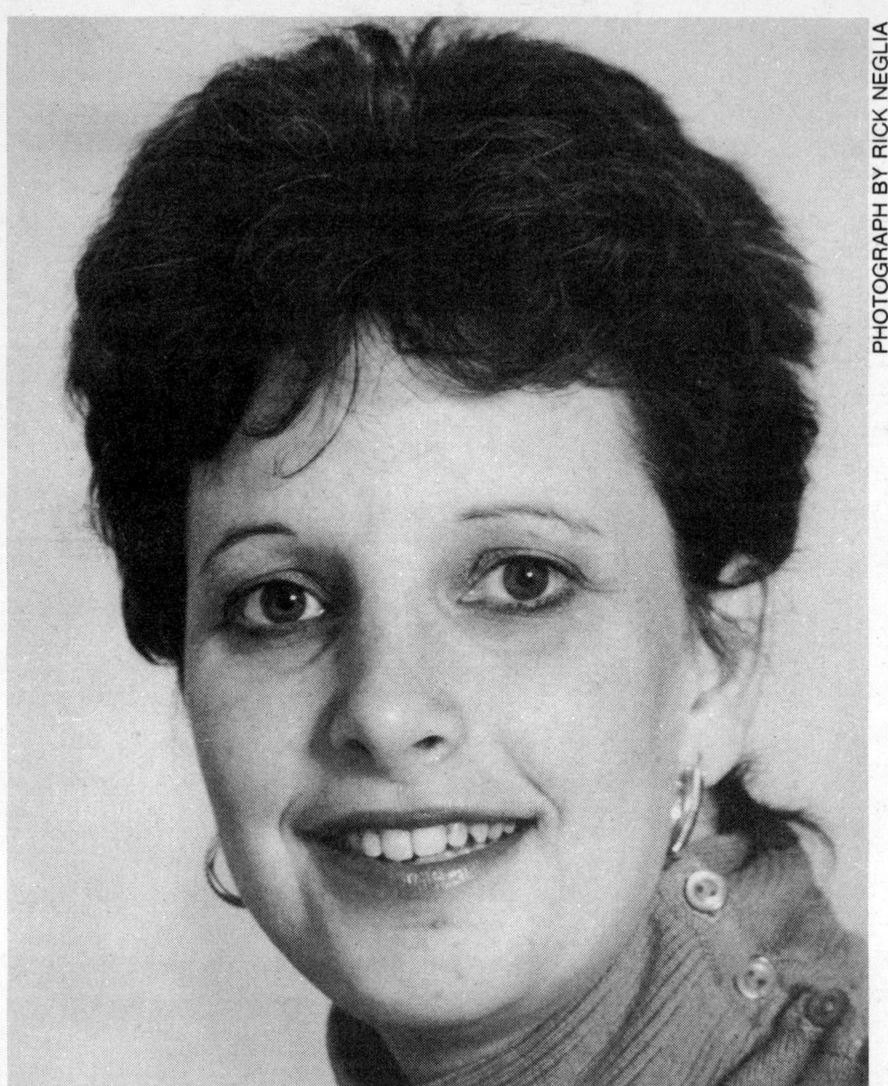

Bev Cline is a Toronto-based freelance writer specializing in business topics, and a contributing editor of *Small Business* magazine. Her work has appeared in many newspapers and magazines, among them, *Toronto Life*, *The Financial Post* and *The Toronto Star* and *The London Free Press*. She is the author of *The Lombardo Story* and *The Terrific Toronto Trivia Book*.